INDIA IN COGNITIVE DISSONANCE

DISSONANCE

A MASTERPIECE ON GEOPOLITICS AND INTERNATIONAL
RELATIONS FROM AN INDIAN PERSPECTIVE

EDITORS OF GREATGAMEINDIA

XpressPublishing
An imprint of Notion Press

XpressPublishing
An imprint of Notion Press

Old No. 38, New No. 6
McNichols Road, Chetpet
Chennai - 600 031

First Published by Notion Press 2020
Copyright © Editors of GreatGameIndia 2020
All Rights Reserved.

ISBN 978-1-64828-323-9

Dedicated to our Teachers — who taught us about Matter, Space and Time —
and intended as a warning to our degenerate society that has separated us from them.

Contents

Preface

For more than 2000 years a war is being waged for the control of India and the access routes connected to it. The Turkey Coup is the beginning of the end of the Great Game, as it is known. With Russia slipping out of their hands, the eyes were set on an unfathomably resource-rich country, which even after thousand years of non-stop plunder and looting still captures the imagination of one and all, thugs, thieves and robber-barons alike with her yet-unknown massive economic resources potential — that country is India.

Let the Indians note that none of the PeethaDhiPatis either of the Vaishnavite or the Shaivite Order or MuttaDhipathis or the Sri Vidya Upasakas or any other Indian Religious Leaders either consciously or unconsciously, either in wakeful state or their dream state, even raise the faintest of protests asking our Government to restore this greatest ancient center of learning where for the first time massive bodies of knowledge were committed to writing.

The main cause of the financial ruin in the interval between 2008 to 2012 was currency manipulation, without any gold left to back it up. If the countries were not of European origin, they are all subjected to what we can now call as Gold Wars or Pipeline Wars in which Iraq and Libya were knocked out and promptly their gold-reserves were confiscated. The world is witnessing the similar brink-of-war situation with the other four powers.

Are schools in India an automated production line converting Indian students to slaves? Don't the managements no longer have the wisdom to think any better? Don't they care whether the children of their schools are called criminals by their own Government? Are the Teacher-Student relations in India not based on fraud?

The Government has built a new IIT at Hyderabad. Did even one responsible citizen of Hyderabad ask: "When we have IITs in India, why is the Black Box of our Late Chief Minister's crashed helicopter being sent to the US for reading? The American education system has already been destroyed by the theories of Sigmund Freud. And that the vast majority of Indians who view America ape precisely this destroyed component. Thus it is that we asked the question: "Time Travel: India 2040 Prime Minister Sigmund Freud?"

Exactly while the corporate-controlled-media used the artificially-created pro-Pakistan ruckus in JNU to divert our attention, our gold-mines have been auctioned away to foreign based companies on the basis of the claim that "India does not have the technology to mine gold". If we can send a mission to Mars, why can't we mine our own gold?

India is rumored to have made great strides in the field of Information Technology — or so we are told. Is the kind of complete negligence, carelessness and shabby-sloppiness exhibited by UIDAI to be the hallmark of Digital India? Did any of India's theoretical physicists provide any input at all on the Quantum Entanglement theory and its role in both cracking the current Cryptographic Keys and in providing an in-theory-un-crackable key to the Aadhaar Project Managers?

Are you aware that one of the key dimensions of the Strategic Defense Initiative required the reduction and degradation of Indian Army from a formidable and feared fighting force, capable of protecting the country from any threat, into a degenerate, fourth-grade and politicized institution?

When India tested the nuclear weapons in Pokhran-II, the only country that congratulated us was France, when everyone else condemned it. What was unique about the French view on India? Did not India's Scientific Establishment have a duty to go on Strike when the head of their own Nuclear Weapons program is called a liar?

A US Trade Official, Carla Hills, had once triggered a massive outrage by calling Indians thieves and criminals. So, are Indians the Thieves of Carla Hills, the Thieves of the Bhagavad Gita or Unique Indian Donkeys of the UID Aadhaar project, or as the author of Mein Kampf would say — are we Rats following the Pied Piper of Hamelin?

India in Cognitive Dissonance is an explosive hard-hitting myth-buster, a timely reminder for the decadent Indian society; a masterpiece on Geopolitics and International Relations from an Indian perspective. It lays bare the hypocrisy that has taken root in the Indian psyche because of the falsehoods that Indian society has come to accept as eternal truth.

CHAPTER ONE

Spokesperson Of Our Nationalist Party Or Good Boy Of England?

The spokesperson of our ruling party, the BJP, had recently given a speech on Foreign Policy in a prestigious University-College in Pune, which is considered to be a premier educational city in India. The spokesperson was also the Nationalist Party's national General Secretary, and who was also an RSS Rashtriya Swayamsevak Sangh pracharak. At the outset, he started off by quoting "Lord" Palmerston and Kissinger in his message to the well-heeled students of this college.

"There are no permanent friends" said he........................."Pragmatism" said he..........................."Hillary Clinton said Look East"..............." so India should Look East" said he....

Did no student of this prestigious college, located in India's premier educational city, ask him any basic question on the history of either Palmerston or Kissinger? If no, **they are not fit to be students.** Students who do not learn by questioning are not worth the money their parents spend on them.

Does the spokesperson know, or does he not know, that Palmerston is a key figure of the historical British Anti-Russia Policy? Does he, or does he not, know that the Palmerston Doctrine is responsible for all the dreadful wars in Central Asia, **including the fragmentation of India?**Does he, or does he not, know that Palmerston played a key role in the Opium Wars that devastated the Chinese people? If he does not, **his advisory group and his speech-preparers are not fit for their job.**

Did no student of International Relations tell the spokesperson that by starting off quoting "Lord" Palmerston and Kissinger and making them the basis of your speech, you are instantly making enemies with both the Russians and the Chinese? If no, **they are not fit to study International Relations.**

Did no Women present there (including the Lady Principal) remind the BJP spokesperson that Kissinger was the one who had used filthy, unspeakable language against our own Woman Prime Minister (Madam Indira Gandhi) in the context of her protecting India in the 1971 war? Did no Women present there tell him that to quote Kissinger inside India – that too on foreign Policy- would be an appalling insult to Mrs. Indira Gandhi as well as to all the Women of India? If no, **these are Women who are not fit to follow the footsteps of Mrs. Indira Gandhi...**What a shame on them!

Did no RSS rashtriya "swayamsevak" politely tell the BJP spokesperson that instead of quoting Palmerston and Kissinger, he ought to quote an Indian Authority on International Relations. Or shamelessly do they admit that we have no such authority at all? At least being a RSS-pracharak he could have quoted Hedgewar or Golwalkar. If no, **they are not fit to be "swayamsevaks"**...whatever this word might mean.

Did not the head of the RSS Rashtriya Swayamsevak Sangh, discuss this matter with the spokesperson? If no, the **RSS ought to question whether any blood is flowing to its head,** unless of course RSS Rashtriya Swayamsevak Sangh stands for either "Rashtriya-Stupid-Sangh" or for "Royal-Sevak-Sangh of Her Majesty the Queen of England"—which it more likely is; or a combination of both—which it certainly is.

The Defense Minister had attended the birthday party of the RSS head. While spending time with the birthday-boy, did he discuss the matter with head of the RSS Rashtriya Swayamsevak Sangh? The spokesperson had said in the same speech that China is militarily far ahead of India, is then creating an open enmity with both China and Russia not a concern referable to the Defense Ministry? Should not the Defense Minister take note and correct both the spokesperson and the RSS-chief? If no, **who else should be correcting the RSS Rashtriya Swayamsevak Sangh chief on this?**

Did no "Indian-pragmatist" tell this gentleman that suggesting that "India should look East" because "Mrs. Hillary Clinton says so", may not be so pragmatic after all, since Mrs. Clinton had just lost the election and is potentially facing serious charges? And anyway, shortly thereafter UNESCAP, the UN-controlled body would ask India to start looking west. Did no "Indian-pragmatist" tell this spokesperson that Kissinger had supported everything that Trump had campaigned against, and that he was against everything that Trump had campaigned for? Although of course Kissinger and Trump would finally anyway work together to make America a Great Nation (which it should be), quoting Kissinger at this juncture, could potentially antagonize Trump?

Did no Indian-pragmatist tell this gentleman that the Americans are far more adept at the art of Pragmatism than the Indians are? Pragmatism is for people who know who they are, know what they want, know what they can do, and how to avoid themselves being destroyed by it. It is not for a country or people whose spokesman posits himself on the quotes of "Lord" Palmerston and Kissinger, and suggesting that India should look East because Hillary Clinton said so – without even knowing the basic history of these figures. That we are in no condition to play this game of Pragmatism, and if we try to do so, **we will be wiped out**, not to mention be hated the world over – as we already are for our wishy-washy stand on several international issues? If no, **they are no Indians fit to be "pragmatists"**.

In the 1971 war, India was about to be trisected and torn apart by the American Seventh Fleet from the East, the Royal Navy from the West and by the Kissinger-instigated Chinese from the North, when we were moments away from destruction, it was the Silent Russians who decided "we cannot stand by and watch our Indian friends be destroyed" and ringed us with their submarines and averted our destruction. And this BJP spokesperson says "we have no friends" while simultaneously quoting Palmerston and Kissinger who are not only the arch-enemies of the Russians but also those who have also divided and destroyed us?

Did no moral authority in India tell this spokesperson of our National Ruling Party that it is the **height of shamelessness** for India to take this position? If no, **then no one is fit to be a moral authority in India.**

Within hours of Turkish Prime Minsiter Erdogan regaining control in the coup-attempt against by in Turkey last year, by the followers of Fetullah Gulen, Turkish authorities contacted India in an attempt to control the followers of Fetullah Gulen, who they knew or claimed are sheltered in vast numbers inside India. Both the Turkish Ambassador to India as well as the Turkish Foreign Minister had met with the head of our MEA and requested that the followers of Fetullah Gulen who are being sheltered in India be sent back to Turkey.

What are we hearing?? That India is the main bastion for the followers of the Fetullah Gulen movement which incited the coup in Turkey? To have been able to instigate and start the coup in Turkey, it must have been a very large organization, built over several years. Since how long have the followers of Fetullah Gulen been entering India? On what passports, on what visas have they entered? Who is giving them shelter? How are the funds reaching them? How are they communicating back with their control centers? Where are their control centers? Are we going to say the control centers are in Pakistan? Have they been issued Aadhaar cards? They are known to have infiltrated several of the institutions of the Turkish society, including the army, the judiciary, the universities etc..What would be then their predicted behavior in the much softer Indian society? In addition to the followers of the Fetullah Gulen Movement, which other organizations involved in the middle-eastern quagmire have their followers being given shelter in India? **Did no Student ask any such question? Did no Faculty member there ask any such question?** What are the moral issues involved in giving them sanctuary? Or to be "pragmatic", to use the same words of the spokesperson, what is the danger that giving them shelter poses to the Indian Society?

The Indian people had to hear this for the first time from the Turkish Ambassador and then the Turkish Foreign Minister? Did not a single member of our Internal Home Security bring this to our attention before the Turks did? Did nobody from the RAW, the Home Ministry, or the MEA warn the people of India or their elected leaders?

It would seem that our Internal Security needs significant overhauling. Or should we assume as the MEA seems to suggest—without and proof, reason or discussion — that the Turkish Ambassador and the Turkish Foreign Minister are lying? What do the Turks benefit by lying on this count? Even if we do not believe the input from the Turkish Ambassador or Foreign Minister, is it not the duty of the Internal Home Ministry to increase the investigation into this matter? Or is the complete Political Security Establishment as well as the Internal Security Establishment party to this matter? Yes, for safety reasons, it may be true that the Internal Security Apparatus may claim that they cannot publicly speak about these details, but this rule does not apply to the other sections of society. Anyway, the fate of their "classified" dossiers is shown below.

The ludicrousness of the MEA's premise that Turkey has not provided enough evidence, is its mirror image in the Indian question to Pakistan: The Pakistanis have long been asking the Indians for solid evidence in the 26/11 case, Samjhauta case, the Malegoan blasts; and has then stated exactly what the Indian MEA said to Turkey: "India has not provided us with any critical evidence so we can't prosecute them." And on the basis of this, most Indians in righteous indignation think that the Pakistanis are liars and Indians accuse the Pakistanis of sheltering the terrorists and lying about it on top of that. Well, can't Turkey make exactly the same accusation against India — That India is harboring ISIS terrorists and telling lies to the rest of the world about it? The "classified" dossier but by now publicly available, (speaks volumes of the safety of our classified documents!!) of the evidence provided by the Government of India on these issues looks like a childish joke, bordering on the parameters of extreme naivete or of intellectual-cognitive dissonance.

But did the either the students or the faculty members of this elite International University at Pune, ask the BJP spokesperson, who is also the National General Secretary of the party, any question regarding this very dangerous phenomenon that is not coming from the region where he said the future dynamics belongs? If no, as said earlier, **they are not fit to be students, nor are the faculty members fit to be faculty members.**

This spokesperson instead of showing his party as a Nationalist Party that stands for a strong and independent India has instead created the tragic projection: **BJP=British Janissary Party.**

Let us now turn away from him. After all, this poor ill-advised gentleman may be the spokesperson of our ruling party, but still he is not all of India.

CHAPTER TWO

Information Technologists Or Ill-Informed Monkeys?

India is rumored to have made great strides in the field of Information Technology — or so we are told. While the public is treated to Big Words such as: "continuously updating security parameters" and "threats in cyberspace", the ground reality seems to be rather different. Well, in the interests of our National Security, let us take a closer look.

We please urge our reader to refer a statement issued by the UIDAI itself, for example in New Indian Express dated 5 March 2017.

Statement by UIDAI as reported by New India Express 5 March 2017 :-

"The UIDAI, the statement stated, is continuously updating its security parameters looking at the new threats in cyber space. "It also undertakes security audits and takes necessary steps to augment its security features. *UIDAI has decided to have registered devices for capturing biometrics data and further that such biometrics will be encrypted at the point of capture itself.* This will further strengthen the security features of the UIDAI Aadhaar eco-system ..the statement added." (Italics mine)

Well, do we wake up in March of 2017 to hear the UIDAI telling us that it has decided to have registered devices for capturing biometric and that further it going to start encrypting the biometrics from the point of capture itself. **DO THEY EVEN REALIZE THE IMPLICATIONS OF WHAT THEY ARE SAYING AND ADMITTING TO?**

So then are we hearing that in the Year of the Lord Jesus Christ, 2017, the UIDAI of the Most Prestigious UIDAI Aadhaar Project of India woke up to the realization that data should be encrypted from the point of capture itself, and that you need to register the devices on which the Biometrics are being collected??

It took them several years to come to this realization?? While, as they claim they may have encrypted the biometrics data of Indians while it is inside their database, where it is relatively more secure, and shout "our databases are highly secure", **are we to conclude from their own statement that they are themselves admitting that they DID NOT ENCRYPT THE biometric data of 1.1 billion Indians at the most vulnerable points (where the encryption is much more required!!). They are going to start doing it now?? ...What were they doing UPTO NOW?–and they are themselves thus admitting that the Biometric data of 1.1 billion Indians was collected on un-registered devices that they did not know about? And then not encrypted immediately..??** Then at what point in the data flow path did they start the encryption?? How did they ensure that they have deleted the data immediately after encryption from the flow-path sections prior to the encryption– before it could be siphoned off by un-scrupulous elements in the earlier segments of the flow-path? From the standpoint of security theory, if security-critical data has been sent on any segment of the architecture without encryption, **it should be treated as security-compromised.**

This is what they themselves are admitting to...... If they committed this kind of a blunder in the initial architecture, should they have been careful to keep quiet about it? Or should they have by mistake have "admitted it", that too after the data of 1.1 billions Indians should from the security standpoint be treated as security-compromised? What punishment should they themselves be given under the Aadhaar Act 2016? What sort of a joke is this?

If they have committed this kind of an architectural-design mistake, what other mistakes have they committed?

Did not even one single one of the millions of these IT-professionals in the country **catch this serious, un-pardonable breach of security?** Are you telling us that the biometrics of 1.1 billion Indians could have been lifted off from the point of collection itself? That they were not encrypted immediately? Fingerprints – which can be easily replicated using hardware and software and a polymer for a few dollars –can be obtained, of millions Indians, just from about any collection center? Is that what they themselves are telling us?? When the rest of the world is moving away from Biometrics, why did we not see the numerous studies on this issue done by the West raised by our Indian IT-professionals? If no, they are not fit to be called IT-professionals. **Shame on all the so-called IT-professionals of India....**

It is public knowledge that the American Firm Price Waterhouse Coopers was given the job of looking into the Security aspect of this project, again by their own statements. Please, Please, **may we let these pitiable Indian IT-experts — wearing coats, driving Mercedes-Benz**, staying in seven star hotels while Indian farmers are committing suicide at a rate of 30 persons per-day — please know that **Cryptographic Security issues for US-Government computers** should be checked via a standard called the **"Federal Information Processing Standards."** All systems belonging to or purchased by any US-governmental organization MUST meet these standards. Is it surprising (or not surprising?) if the Indian UIDAI project did not follow the same standard, given it was audited by an American Firm. The more general security (not exclusively to Cryptography) should meet what are called **"Common Criteria Standards"**. These standards span not only the US, but most countries in the world.

Please, may we bring to the notice of our abominably-**ill-informed Indian readers** who fight like un-educated goons, and **so-called IT-experts** who may have debated this matter, **that there is no such thing as "Secure" or "Insecure"**. There is such a thing as "Secure at Evaluated Assurance Level -1" or **"Secure at Evaluated Assurance Level-4"**. Level-1 maybe OK for your home, Level 7 would be for Governmental Security Computers. You cannot simply shout... "WE ARE SECURE" .... "oh no, YOU ARE NOT SECURE." This makes Indians look like CAVEMEN — the world already thinks so anyway.

Please, may we tell our readers, that there SHOULD be a document called the **"Security Target"**, amongst others that should be made AVAILABLE TO THE PUBLIC. This "Security Target" document should contain a "complete list of ALL the Security Claims being Made." **For all security certifications, in the USA and Europe, including that of the high security servers, these documents are PUBLICLY AVAILABLE on the certifier's website.**

We would then have expected at least a few thousand questions based on this from our Indian IT-experts. For, these tragic folk, let take it on ourselves to provide a few examples. A level of detail for cryptography question would be: **"Is the Random-Number-Generator (used for the encryption key creation) actually generating random numbers? or are they not actually random..** in which case, the encryption Key can be easily broken".......all the way from this level of detail.....to an intermediary level: **"Prove that no process running on the system is transmitting data outside** the system"........ To a far more outer-layer questions such as : **"What is the Electromagnetic Emission signature of the device?"; Can data can be accidentally sent-out via the electromagnetic emission?** " to personnel handling protocols: **"Who has access to the Device Under test?**And What Physical Protocols do they follow when entering and leaving the room..such as **check for no pen-drives or other storage devices in the pocket** of any and all entering the room". These and thousands of others like this one should have publicly debated by our IT-establishment, and the results should be PUBLICLY AVAILABLE.

But **if as you say, you have been using devices that are not registered, we cannot even think of asking any of these security-related questions?**If you cannot ask any security-related questions, how do you start thinking about security? Then What Security in Heaven's name are you talking about?? **IIT-JEE rank number -1 usually picks Computer Science as first choice, and not one question of this kind is seen from the entire spectrum of the IIT-trained computer scientists?**

The answers to all these questions should be in the Public Domain, available for public inspection via the internet. This is the way it is done for all devices purchased by the US government. **Are the Security Target, the Proof-structures for the Security-Claims, etc** for this UID project **in the Public Domain as they should be??**

Are they not OR Are they? Let us look at the implications of both cases:-

Case 1) If They ARE NOT on the Public Domain: If they are not in the Public Domain, then there is absolutely NO PROOF of any claim of the UID-project security, and however much they shout, it has to be taken that the UID-project is completely and totally devoid of any security, and it would have been the **duty of the so-called IT-experts** in the country to bring to the notice of the Learned Chief Justice and of the Public that if these documents were not made available for Scrutiny and **it be would the Universally Accepted Case that the UID project must be taken as having no security protocols at all**... universally.... minus cognitive-dissonant India...that is.

OR

Case 2) If They ARE in the Public Domain: If they are on the public domain easily available on the internet, then Please May we politely ask, why in this entire debate that was witnessed in India spanning the past several years, **NOT ONE SINGLE PERSON, NOT THE IT-MINISTER, NOT ONE SINGLE IT-EXPERT, NOT EVEN THE LEARNED CHIEF**

JUSTICES asked the First-Question that should be asked:- "**WHERE IS YOUR SECURITY TARGET POLICY DOCUMENT?**" which contains your "SECURITY CLAIMS"? **WHERE IS YOUR LINKING DOCUMENT** Linking the SECURITY CLAIMS WITH THE SECURITY REQUIREMENTS? **WHERE ARE YOUR TEST RESULTS?**", "**WHERE ARE YOUR ARCHITECTURAL DIAGRAMS?**" ——– these should be Publicly Available on your certifiers website, and should have been shown to all who wanted to see the, as is the case for all secure systems worldwide. NOT your SHOUTING: "We are secure...We are absolutely Secure...We are telling you we are secure!!!" NOT the Learned Chief Justice of the Supreme Court saying: "We can accept the assurances of security given by them".

Did you review your architectural diagrams properly? Did you test whether the encryption is being done where it is actually should be? **If yes, then how, in Dear God's name is this report appearing in the newspaper, by your own spokesperson? What a shame !!!!!**

Granted the common man of India does not the courage or wherewithal to challenge these big words "Internet Security" or "CyberSpace" **but did no coat-tie-wearing CEO of any Indian company**, arriving at his Company in a Mercedes Benz and getting a Salaam from the doorkeeper and Secretaries **have the courage to ask the question the UIDAI:-**

Why in heaven's name did you not discover this error in the early Architectural Stages of your design? Why did you not see this error in you Security Policy Document..which should be Public?

And one fine morning in March 2017, a common Indian citizen wakes up to learn that the data was not being encrypted at the point of capture via a newspaper-carried statement that stated this by inadvertent implication? **Or should we have learnt that the data was not being encrypted from the point of capture via a Test-case-document Review — or more properly from the Architectural Design Review phase itself?** Even a basic glance at international security requirements would make this look like an INTERNATIONAL LAUGHING JOKE, implemented by primitives.

It is hard to understand that after so many Indians have been granted H1-B visas and worked in the USA, and returned to India, since the past 20 years now, this same careless attitude continues. **Not only today, but fifteen years ago in even a petty American IT company, for this kind of a mistake, the Chief Technology Officer would have been immediately fired and he would not have got a job anywhere else.**He would have been laughed at for the rest of his life. What sort of a joke is India's Information-

Technology? No wonder at all that Donald Trump is cutting back on Indian H1-B visas. Perhaps Donald **Trump is doing the right thing in kicking the Indian "IT-experts" out. God Bless America.**

ALL IT-PROFESSIONALS IN INDIA CEOs, CTO,s developers , project-managers etc, etc. as shown above in either case-1 or case-2 your are gone. You are the representatives of "Digital India", the glorious path ahead as indicated by our Honorable Prime Minister. Is this complete negligence, carelessness and shabby- sloppiness exhibited by each and every one of you to be the hallmark of Digital India as envisioned by our Honorable Prime Minister Shri Narendra Modi? You have badly let our Honorable Prime Minister down, as well as endangered the entire country.

The security of our whole country is now at stake. We do not want to hold you responsible for this. But, as has been shown above, your knowledge of the IT field is itself highly questionable. Given this, it is not likely that you understand the fundamentals of any other field in society. Please do your bit to tone down the IT-hype before the entire country is endangered. The more serious question of the security of the most responsible members of our society, including the Prime Minister and RBI chief, will be discussed in a later section.

Contrary to what you may think, We are not pointing fingers exclusively at the UIDAI or at the IT-folk alone; In our next sections we shall attempt to see who is actually responsible this state of affairs.

Perhaps, it is time to take a break, **return to your ancestral homes,** use the money you have earned working as slaves for the IT-sector to buy back the lands you fathers sold away, and **start agriculture again first by LEARNING HOW TO GRAZE YOUR DONKEYS...** don't ask the local farmer's son to do it for you just because you have the money..learn it yourself...nothing wrong with this at all. Oh, by the way don't be scared...you will not be alone in the village!! You will find there your friends from the IIMs waiting for you. Except that instead of grazing donkeys, they will be driving the bullock-carts....Read on the rest of this document. And by the way for those IIM-MBAs who scream: "You will push us back to the dark ages", we have reserved a section on the actual cavemen of India.)

Polite Note to Chief Justices of India.

It should be noted however that the former Chief Justices of the Supreme Court have stood their ground to protect the Indian public, **although they might have seriously erred in "accepting the assurances"** given by the UIDAI regarding security. These issues of Technology are perhaps difficult to grasp given that they are busy with so many other things, and it was upto the IT professionals to educate them. They, the Learned Judges have served their country as well as they could, via the Supreme Court, which any common man in India will tell you has lost most of its relevance. It may be time for them to abandon it to the reality of History. We wish them a happy retirement to their villages where they can perhaps run the more simple village panchayats and pray God to grant them birth in a better society in their next life. **No Punishment that the learned Judges can award is adequate for this crime that has been committed against the people of India.........**

P.S. Request to our Income Tax Authorities of India:

The Income-tax department has been kind in receiving suggestions, and has updated many security practices, based upon inputs from the general public. Please may we bring to the notice of the Income Tax department of India one more shoddy security practice that is still continuing. The Income tax department is sending notices such as ITR-V over the e-mail using for encryption a combination of lower_case PAN number and birthdate (half of the PAN being in the message header and the birthdate being obtainable from the e-mail account). This is poor security practice. **Please may we politely tell the Income Tax department that if you wanted to communicate via e-mail, the correct thing to do, is to send an e-mail containing a message " Notification from Income Tax: Please logon to Income Tax Website to see notification",** do not send any other details via the e-mail. If Individuals can access their e-mail, surely they can logon to the much more secure IncomeTax website, and then download the ITR-V, using for example a simple encryption key that can be set on/from the website. **If there are these kind of poor-security-procedures even as of today, it is likely that there are many other problems as well. It is upto your team to find all of them out. It is very un-fair on your part to expect the hard-working-tax-paying public of India to point all of these out to you.IT** DOES NOT LOOK GOOD ON YOU IF THE COMMON PUBLIC POINTS THEM OUT, although we may not mind doing so.

CHAPTER THREE

Students Of India Or Criminals Of Indian Government?

In addition to the well-known "PRISM" and "Boundless Informant" data mining programs being run the USA, shall we refer the specific targeting of Science and Technology Activities by the US against both India and China? Who in India's establishment should be aware of the US government's doctrine that Data Mining should be proactively used to assist in reducing to fourth-grade the Chinese and Indian scientific establishments? Are the Directors of the IIT's aware of this? If yes, how did they respond? If no, they need to stand up and ask the Government as to why they should not be in the loop on this critical information.

The **biometric data of all the armed forces and defense and police personnel and of the IIT students of India were then transmitted using this shabbily implemented technology which is clearly being controlled by foreign organizations?**The biometric profiles along with all the other linked–databases complete biographic details and profiles of the applicants to the prestigious JEE entrance exam, **the brightest Indian students, who could be our future leaders should be put on public view on the internet** for all to see because of this very shoddy project?

Did not a single member of the Defense chiefs or the Police chiefs realize the danger and press for members of the Armed Forces and the Police to be exempted from the highly dangerous Aadhaar requirement and make the security personnel aware of basics of IT security? Was the investigation into this matter by these esteemed members of our society as shoddy as that of the general public? Do our Defense Chiefs and Police Chiefs know that the more elite units of several countries have been warned to stay completely clear of the internet? If no, **the Defense chiefs and Police chiefs have grossly failed in their duties, and have compromised the security of the country, as well as of the people under their command.**

Did the Directors of the IITs fail to look into this security aspect and take objection to this and ensure that the complete informational profiles of the brightest of our Indian students entering the IITs, who can be our future leaders, are not put in public view for all and sundry? Was the investigation into this matter by the IITs as shoddy as that of the general public? If no, they **have failed in their duty to their students and to their country.**

Did the numerous coaching centers for the IIT preparation object to this? Well, we ignore them..anyway they are limited to selling knowledge for money...they have no sense of duty, nor do they inculcate it in the Indian students.

Did no Bank-Authorities object to this? As explained in the earlier section, following the UIDAI's statement and the internationally accepted security standards for critical-data the biometric data of all which were collected upto now till they can implement the procedures described earlier, should now be treated as security-compromised. **Bank-authorities plan to use these security-compromised-biometrics to handle security in the Indian Peoples Accounts?**They are using this kind of shoddy technology implemented by primitives to play with the money of hard-working-honest Indians? Did no bank-manager ask about the security implications of this project and of using (compromised!)Biometrics—which are anyway being discarded the world over—which can be easily replicated using publicly available software and hardware and some polymer-resin? Even if **many Bank Managers are overloaded, if they don't have the time to understand these issues, they better not use this technology. They clearly need better lessons on security...** they better start asking their own questions. If they cannot escalate the legitimate security concerns of the public, the Indian public will soon start wondering: **"Is our money is safe in these banks...with this kind of pathetic security protocols?"**

Airports in India, which are supposed to have the highest standards of security, are planning to use these security-compromised-biometrics for authenticating airline passengers? Well, people will soon start wondering about their safety, when all biometric-data of 1.1 billion people collected until now is security-compromised as explained earlier.

India is a signatory to the **International Convention on the Rights of the Child**. Regardless of what the Indian Supreme Court thinks about the "right to privacy for Indian Citizens", **privacy of children is protected under Article 16 of this International Convention**. Numerous schools have forced parents and their children to get this highly controversial Aadhaar card and the biometrics of the children were forcibly taken.

Does no lawyer in the country know that it is illegal under international law to obtain biometrics of children–even with the consent of an adult– unless the child has already committed a crime. If no, **they are not fit to be lawyers.**

Did no Indian Parent raise the question of **abysmal immorality** and **internationally-** accepted **illegality of fingerprinting children** who are not confirmed to have already committed a crime? Even the most notorious dictatorial regimes have not stooped to this abysmal depth. If no, **they are not fit to be called parents.**

Did no school Principal raise this same question? Well, we excuse them- they are only cogs in the wheel. Schools in India are the automated production line for the slaves. The managements no longer have the wisdom to think any better. They don't seem to care whether the children of their schools are called criminals by their own Government.

Oh and by the way, the earlier section of the article, we had asked whether the RSS-chief had either issued a reprimand to, or at least discussed with, his RSS Pracharak — the BJP spokesperson — regarding the abysmal immorality and stupidity of quoting Palmerston and Kissinger on a foreign-policy speech. Well, perhaps that may be a little too much to ask of him. After all the RSS bases itself on a philosophy and draws its cadre from those who are called **HINDUS = Her-majesty's INdians DUmb and Stupid.**

Let us suggest to the RSS-chief something more simple – something concerning his own RSS-shakhas. Please issue a request to change one of your phrases: change the phrase "Bachcha Bachcha Raam Hai" to "**Bachcha Bachcha Chor Hai**" – and while you are at it, also change the expansion of RSS to "Rashtriya Stena Sangh". The Queen of England and Prime Minister Theresa May, who was treated as the Goddess herself, by your own priests, would be mighty pleased!!!

CHAPTER FOUR

Quantum Entanglement And The Indian Cavemen

A Mathematical algorithm is used to calculate a number from the iris scan taken during the Aadhaar card application. The Hatha Yoga Pradipika is merely one amongst several ancient Sanskrit texts that mentions the vast amount of information that can be obtained by looking into a person's eye.

Did any of our scholars of Yoga and other "Yogis" who have come out in the public domain, who proudly teach it to the Americans, ask: What information might the process of photographing the iris of all the Indians yield to the highly committed and dedicated American Scientists who will have access to all this data If not, **they are not fit to call themselves Yogis or Yoga teachers**... they are pimps of the Yoga.

Did any single Mathematician from any Indian University ask what may this algorithm be and what information can be obtained from it? If no, **they better stop doing Mathematics**. They do injustice to Math and the country also does injustice to them.

Encryption is a theory that uses advanced fields of Mathematics. Few, if any, Indians are aware that most of the **Ramanujan equations were hidden away by the British** and were then used to break the codes of the German Enigma machines in the early stages of encryption technology, which was then used to destroy the complete U-boat fleet and keep the Allied ships away from them. **In a very good sense therefore, it would not be completely unfair to say that the Indian Scientific Establishment is forced to speak English today, only because of cracking of Cryptographic codes!!**

Did any Indian mathematician ask the simple obvious question: If, as is commonly known, the British kept Ramanujan with them, why would they release all of his equations to the rest of the world, what major part are they still holding and **can they use this to crack our Encryption, and provide this information to this UID-debate?**

Did any Indian Mathematician studying Cryptography (how many do?) ask to inspect the so-called high-quality encryption of this Aadhaar Project? We boast that **Srinivasa Ramanujan is an Indian Mathematical genius,** but the Supreme Court had to ask foreign opinion on the matter...Did no Mathematician from any Indian University give his opinion on this public debate? If no, **they ought to abandon Mathematics.** They cannot use it for a higher purpose.

Did anyone of India's theoretical physicists provide any input at all on the quantum entanglement theory and its role in both cracking the current Cryptographic Keys and in providing an in-theory-un-crackable key to the Aadhaar Project Managers, and help them to understand the issue, intead of letting them implement what is shown above have implemented what is an international joke? If no — well, for this once let us not blame the theoretical physicists, **because understanding quantum entanglement is way too much for the pathetic and vain-glorious figures of the IT field** who are may have been involved in the implementation this project; we do not think it even worth to ask the converse: Did any of these project managers ask you for your input?

Did even one single Minister of our IT-crazed society ask, that if IT is the way of the future (and with the shout and scream of "data security" jarring our ears rather than driving our minds), shouldn't we ministers be abreast of the fields in this area? With a revolutionary technology already being implemented by the Chinese, perhaps we should avoid wasting Thousands of Crores on a technological project that will be in a very short while obsolete? Shall we mention here the fact that a **Chinese Satellite, using this theory, is already in orbit** — **teleporting data via quantum-cryptography?**If no, **they are not fit to be Ministers.**

We do not wish to scare our lotus-eating Indians with ideas such as Reverse Engineering of the Brain, Genetic Algorithms, Directed Evolution, Cognitive Modeling, Electromagnetic-field-based Viruses for the Human Mind, Psychotronic Viruses, Remote Cerebral Control, virtual reality and neural computer interfacing. The terms neural- and bio- telemetry, bioenergetics, bioelectromagnetic nonthermal interactions, telecybernetics, Radio Frequency weapons, radionics, remote brain wave monitoring, can be seen in more than just one of the Western defense journals today. Several Western Defense publications will tell even a cursory reader that the acronym BRAIN stands for Biometric Recognition and Identification Network of the CIA, NSA and the DOD.

While we certainly do not wish to panic-monger, our Defense Minister should at least be aware of these terms. Why then did our leading scientific establishments not provide even the most basic information about these terms in the Indian public debate? These issues need to be investigated by a strong, vibrant and well-guided scientific establishment. Did our Defense Ministers enquire on the investigation of these matters with our HRD ministers, the current HRD Minister being eulogized by our media which tells the Indian public ".... he has seen it all starting with student agitations?" Did we hear "Student Agitations"? PLEASE FOR GOD's sake, these things cannot be understood by agitating students, unless he is somehow implying that the student-agitations were themselves caused by remote-control of their brains !!! Hopefully, by now at least our readers should understand that this is very possible. Alas, but our reader should have realized that HRD stands for Her-majesty's Reusable/Recycleable Donkeys.

What kind of a tragic joke is it, in this configuration of things, when our Finance Minister announces in the Rajya Sabha that firewalls will be used to guarantee our data-security in the year 2017?? **Did our Defense Minister not SCREAM–SCCCRREEAAMM–at him** for talking thus? If he did not, then those of whose who still have some semblance of a brain left cannot help but **wonder whether our Defense Minister himself is a zombie created by the project MKULTRA** (quite a few of whose operatives are publicly known to have lived in India), which has been known since the 1950s?

"It is SECURE!" —"No, it is NOT secure!" –I am telling you it is Secure — No, I AM telling you it is NOT —Hoi Hoi Hoi, I am telling you it is Secure!! "NOO, IT IS NOT Secure"—-Hoi Hoooi Hoooi....Maaro Saale Ko.

Thus do we identify the CAVEMEN OF INDIA, fit to be ruled again by the British.

CHAPTER FIVE

Are Indians Donkeys Or Rats Or Thieves of Carla Hills? Fingerprint The Thieves!

The CEO of Google an IIT-Kharagpur Alumni visited the IIT Kharagpur and spoke before a large audience. It is reasonably well known in American circles that several **key appointees to the Google are done directly by the CIA**(not circuitously and in-directly as is their standard operating procedure).

Did even one student of IIT-Kharagpur ask, with the intention of learning, him a question on the open link between the CIA and the Google? Did anyone ask him a question as to why Indians cannot demand from their Government and why India cannot set up its own version of Google? Did the Director of the IIT-Kharagpur think it fit to ask these questions? If no, **the students of the prestigious IIT-Kharagpur either are not there to serve our country or are not fit to be students.** Public money has been wasted on them.

Did we need to wait for newspapers to announce the Snowden (Whose asylum-application India rejected) leaks to tell us that the smartphones and smart TVs can be used as remotely controlled spying devices by a foreign establishment? Do we need to wait till 2013, for the Snowden files to tell us that India was the number-1 target for the American NSA's snooping? Do we need to wait till November 2016 for foxnews to warn us that Android phones are sending data to China. What does this speak about the foresight of our social guidance? We heard pathetic Rajya Sabha members discussing about putting firewalls around the UIDAI servers. What firewalls?? Did any IIT-student of computer science tell his Head of Department to Escalate to the IIT-Director that all major firewalls have been broken into since the late

1990s? That the word "Firewall" has no meaning in any important security matter today?

Did the students of the IITs not ask their professors as to what might be the social impact of these foreign-made devices on the Indian society or why we could not make them in India to the result that India had to import them in such large numbers? If no, **the students of the IITs need additional help on the role of Science and Technology in society, in addition to being taught that the IITs should serve our country's needs first.**

Did any Indian Chartered Accountant ask and find out how it is that if Google, WhatsApp, Facebook etc are offering services "for free", then how are they recovering the hundreds of billions of dollars being spent on their establishments, and caution the Indian public about using these "Free Gifts"? If no, **they are not fit to be chartered accountants.** Did the Institute of Chartered Accountants discuss the matter of accounting concerning this major social issue? No? Then whom are they Accounting? And whom are they Accountable to?

Did no responsible member of the "Spiritual Exalted Sections of our Society" that claim to lead the rest of the society ask the basic moral question and do their duty by telling the society: Just because something is offered "for free" — that does not mean that we should take it? They are lending credence to an oft-heard comment:- **"Udhar Khaana Muft Mey Mil Raha Hai....Toh jaroor Sharmaji udhar hee gaye Honge"**

A US Trade Official, Carla Hills, had once triggered a massive outrage by calling Indians thieves and criminals. **Fingerprint all the Thieves and Criminals !!......**Is this not exactly one of the achievements of the Aadhaar? **We have, by our actions, seemingly agreed to what Carla Hills had said: Indians are Thieves and Criminals.**

Did none of these so-called Bhagavad Gita Exponents, Saraswatis, Aanandas, ..this ji and ...that ji... put into practical application the excerpt (3.12) from the Bhagavad Gita using the Loukika translation: "He who takes from them, without returning to them ought..he verily is called a Thief." Have we not proved, by our own scripture that we Indians are thieves? For our readers, this is the Loukika Translation which they themselves teach. **Where are these fit-for-nothing Bhagavad Gita Exponents?**Have they run away?

Let us put before our reader one of the "relatively smaller" consequences of shoddy computer-security practices in our Indian war history.

During the height of the Kargil war the Army had requested to the Western Naval Command to blockade the Karachi Port in an attempt to release the pressure on the Kargil front. A few Indian submarines headed for Karachi under complete radio silence. They were given double-encrypted codes, until they received a signal that matched any of these, they were to continue on the mission. Before they completed the mission, they somehow received exactly these same codes and returned to base — much to the surprise of the shocked Western Naval Command. The Western Naval Command then checked with Naval HQ in Delhi, who confirmed that they had not sent the codes. To the utter surprise of the Admiralty, nobody knew what was happening. So then to finish the Kargil war, because the Navy could not complete its task of relieving pressure by blockading Karachi, the Air-Force was now pushed towards Operation Safed Sagar.

Following the war a detailed enquiry was launched, whereby it was found that the American Embassy in Delhi (a top secret NSA spy hub codename DAISY) had sent the codes, because America did not want the war to escalate, wanting instead to protect their vassal state of Universal Terrorism (aka Pakistan) and keep it for the purpose of battering Russia. **It was such a complete embarrassment to both the Government of India and to the Armed Forces – they prefer not talk about this issue anywhere.** The GOI then allocated a budget of 2500 crores to insulate the Naval computers from this kind of un-authorized hacking.

Given the experience India has had during the naval war when our double-encrypted naval codes being broken by the American Embassy, we would have thought that far more critical steps would have been taken on the question of cyber-security. However, the public of India, across the spectrum as seen above is simply unable to assist its Government in implementing this, instead is dancing to the tune of slogans being pushed on our well-meaning but powerless MPs by the corporate forces.

A similar affair happened when a massive cyber-attack interrupted and stalled temporarily the military and civilian infra-structure of Iran. But fortunately the Russians were able to detect it and they were able to prevent critical damage to the facility. It is now well known that this attack was jointly carried by Israeli and American intelligence agencies. Let us provide another illustration of the dangers of this.

As recently as few days ago, a North Korean Ballistic Missile Test failed within seconds of take off. Interestingly the British Foreign Secretary has revealed in a Public Press conference, that the failure was due to the massive cyber-attacks launched by American Intelligence Agencies. **Should this not be a warning to our IT-crazed society?** With what we have seen in the UIDAI affair, what do we think is likely to be our fate?

So too, **any missiles or missile-components developed outside India could fail at the most critical moment** because some geopolitical player may not like India defending herself against terrorism which they themselves have sponsored This failure of critical defense equipment at the critical juncture will surely cause immense civilian and military casualties of un-imaginable proportions, and could well lead to the utter and humiliating defeat of India, even at the hands of rag-tag armies or terrorists.

But what have we done? We have proudly announced recently that we are giving a contract worth two-billion dollars for the development of missiles to Israel, ostensibly to fill up the gap in our missile-defense? We forget our DRDO which has put in very good effort to build the excellent ballistic missiles and they are working on intercept missiles as part of our missile shield. We have spent Rs 59,000 crores importing the Raphael jets from France, and then given another Rs 14,000-crore contract to Israel to design the headgear for these jets. **It would seem that we trust Israeli Scientists but not our own, choosing instead to fingerprint and biometrically-tag our own scientists as if they were thieves.**

If these two billion dollars were given to DRDO, probably they could have made the best of the best ballistic missiles and missile shields in less than 5 years, which could be shielded from the cyber-or-on-board-computer attacks when we really needed to use them.

Where are our so-called "Economists", who shout about creating jobs? Well, let them know that according to a United Nations Report itself, every billion dollar investment into any country's economy will create 25,000 high-technology, high-paid permanent jobs. Somehow, unfortunately, this did not sink into our public which resonates to the **"Digital India" slogan, when each and every digital component** starting from **cell-phones to chargers to computers, to laptops** to anything called digital **is imported from various foreign countries**, draining our valuable resources. Not to mention that this has simultaneously **completely destroyed one of our premier Electronics and Digital Research Institute** set up 40 years ago by the Government of India **to help both our defense and civilian digital and electronic infrastructure** (the ECIL, Electronic Corporation of India Limited).

But given the recent WikiLeaks revelation about CIA access to Aadhaar database and **given the pathetic Indian Societal understanding of security issues** as seen in this abominable Aadhaar affair, **we can absolutely be sure that the CIA, NSA and NGI** (the NGI is far more powerful than the NSA) **are listening to anything and everything going on anywhere inside India,** including inside all its military and security establishments. Their motto: **"Your data is our data, your equipment is our equipment – anytime, any place, by any legal means"**Do you think India can match this kind of determination with the condition we are in as described above? Let us quote an internal guideline of a well-known Intelligence Establishment to its trainees: **"If you pay more than 100 Rupees to get information from India, you are not fit to be our officer".**

So, **are Indians the Thieves of Carla Hills, the Thieves of the Bhagavad Gita or Unique Indian Donkeys of the UID Aadhaar project, or as the author of Mein Kampf would say — are we Rats following the Pied Piper of Hamelin???**

CHAPTER SIX

Indian Nuclear Weapons Or Indian Firecrackers?

When India tested the nuclear weapons in Pokhran-II, the only country that congratulated us was France, when everyone else condemned it.

Did any student of India's Physics departments walk across the campus and ask the History Departments in their Universities what was unique about the French view on India? Did the Head of the Departments of Physics ponder on the question and issue instructions to Physics students going abroad for higher studies to go to France instead of all students going to English-speaking America? If no, **they have failed in their administrative duty as Heads of the Indian Physics departments and have not guided the students and faculty properly.**

Students at the IIT are too young — you say? We shall remind our reader that the **modal age of Scientists on the Manhattan Project was a mere 24 years**, by which age they already knew what their country was, why and whom they were fighting with and how best they could serve their country.

Did any History Professor ask and answer this same question? If no, **they are not fit to be Professors of History.**

Did any Political Science Professor ask and answer this same question? If no, **they are not fit to be Professors of Political Science.**

If the Directors of the IITs were told that the IITs are producing highly trained slaves for the Anglo-Saxon lobby, would they be able to debate this matter? Other than knowing that "Anglo-Saxon" has something to do with a Germanic invasion of England in some past time, would they know anything else in this regard. If they Directors of the IITs were asked a simple question: " Is or is not the Indian Scientific Establishment in Anglo-Saxon orbit, and if so (a) should you and (b) how will you pull it out?" Will even a single IIT-Director be able to debate this matter? If no, **the Directors of the IITs** had better sit down to their studies and take some courses in History and Political Science.

The yield of the first French nuclear fission test conducted in the year 1960 was 65 KT. Decades after this, the yield of India's nuclear fusion test (which should be several **hundreds of times more than a fission test**), was less than this figure. This is information obtainable in the public domain...no profound nuclear-weapon calibration secrets here. **What???** **Our nuclear fusion-yield is less than their fission-yield – that too of a test they did decades ago?**

Did anyone of India's investigative reporters splashing this news on the cover pages, stand up and tell our government and our ecstasy-induced euphoric dancing public that a Fusion Weapon capability should be tested and demonstrated in the Mega-ton range, not the Kilo-Ton range? Did anyone of our defense analysts point this simple fact out to our government and tell our Government to conduct the tests in the Mega-Ton range? That the Chinese (for example) have tested the nuclear weapon in multiple battle-scenarios, including 47 tests using air-drop, parachuting, missile-mated, tower-based and atmospheric in addition to the mere underground testing done by India? **That this underground nuclear weapon testing at such low yield is pathetically inadequate for our National Security?** We may be able to launch a ballistic missile, but has the nuclear-weapon warhead been tested in missile-mated configuration or in air-dropped configuration? If no, **they are not fit to be Defense Analysts or Investigative Journalists.**

We might hear that nuclear weapon testing can be simulated on computers using some critical information which is slightly hard, but not impossible to obtain.

Did any member of our Indian Public or Defense Chiefs of Staffs (who may have been fortunate enough to hear of this), ask the question: "Can the Nation be plunged into nuclear war on the basis of nuclear-weapon configurations tested only in Computer Simulations?" If no, **they are not fit to be Defense Chiefs of Staff** and the "educated" **Indian Public who have blindly trusted them,** but did not take the responsibility to ask this same question as a duty to the **simpler-folk of our society, might as well be vaporized via nuclear war.**

About 8 years ago, the Indian National Security Advisor had publicly called a leading core member of the Indian nuclear weapon program a LIAR. **Did not India's Scientific Establishment have a duty to go on Strike** when the head of their own establishment is called thus?Or, if the accusation were in-fact true, did the Establishment consider closing down?

Please may we bring to the notice of the Indian public that the claims made by our Nuclear-Weapon Establishment could potentially be as fraudulent as the claims made by the other establishments. It is your duty to verify the claims by third parties. This is the basis of "Participatory Democracy".. a theory which is well-credited to Muammar Gaddafi of Libya. **Please may we tell you that while Indian reports stated that the yield of the first test in Pokhran-1 was about 8-10 Kt, it is heard from credible sources inside the American establishment, it is actually closer to only 2Kt.**

India had better make up its mind on a choice: either give up nuclear weapons completely (and change the three Lions to three Pussycats) OR **Ensure that the scientists can Test the Nuclear weapons Publicly and Properly in all required configurations.** If you decided on the second path, please make sure that your Scientists can go to the test site in full dignity as Scientists, not carried there hidden in disguise.

Does the reader of this article realize by now that by following the British Pied-Piper there is a real possibility of being pushed into nuclear war—for which we are woefully and hopelessly un-prepared? If no, **you are not fit to read this article — stop right here.**

CHAPTER SEVEN

"Aren't You Ashamed Of Yourself?" From Joseph Stalin To Vijaya Lakshmi Pandit

We had heard the slogan "Gujarat Shining", the actual developments being in great part due to the great efforts of our Prime Minister Honorable Narendra Modi. Very few people indeed have had the privilege of serving both their home state and then the Nation in the manner of our Honorable Prime Minister, Shri Narendra Modi. The population of Gujarat is about 67 million. The population of France is also about 67 million.

It is by now common knowledge that critical signature details of the Scorpene Submarines that we purchased from France were leaked to the whole world before even the first submarine arrived in India. The leak occurred when very irregular companies were used to translate the Submarine's Documents from French into English. What?? India wants its critical military security documents translated from French to English!! What a shame on us.

Did any single Educationist from Gujarat observe: "French Scientists and Engineers can study Science in French and their Submarine design documents and war-plane design documents are in French" and ask "Gujarat has a population equal to that of France. With our Chief Minister now being the Prime Minister why cannot Gujarat — with a population equal to that of France — run a good quality Scientific Establishment and design a submarine and fighter planes, all done in the Gujarati Medium? Certainly Prime Minister Narendra Modi will help us with this effort, after all, Gujarati is his mother tongue and he was our Chief Minister as well." If no, **this is an opportunity they have lost to improve the status and condition of their own langauge**...Anyway, if all the major Scientific

Establishments in Gujarat were operating in English, they would to have been aware of the English short-story whose moral is oft quoted as: **"Do not try to Shine in Borrowed Feathers"**. And they would have instantly seen the problem with the slogan "Gujarat Shining"; and they themselves would have requested that this slogan is actually better not used. The fact that they did not see the problem is indicative of something missing. This something is precisely stemming from the cognitive dissonance that has overtaken us.

The **British Council Report on English as a medium of instruction** notes: "There is an English language policy in schools in the National Curriculum Framework and the Position Paper on English in Schools, but **no such document or thinking exists for higher education in India.**"

WHAT? No thinking exists for higher education in India???

Did any educationist ask "Why does India not have any document or thinking as regards the use of English in its higher Education". Doesn't this imply that we Indians are running our higher education without thinking? If no, **there is no educationist worth the name in India at all.**

India has several Universities that have English departments and there are even complete governmental establishments exclusively for English. Most of them, when asked about the origins and history of the English Language can do little more than mention the Anglo-Saxon invasion of England.

Did any single English Language Professor in India study the origins and the original English Language (which we may tell our reader hardly bears resemblance to the present day English), and use this to predict the future of the English Language and advise the Indian Scientific Establishment which is today operating in English, as to what may be the global future of English and what steps are appropriate for us in the regard? Do we have any Political Scientists studying the international dimensions of the language question, and if so, did they help in this process? If no, **we do not have any single scholar of English of any use to our society at all, nor do we have any scholars of International Relations worth the name.**

Have the Directors of our Research Establishments properly answered the following questions regarding the use of the English language and clearly written position papers on the same- What is the impact of running the Scientific Establishment in English on our social fabric? What is the impact of English on the mind of a student whose mother-tongue is not English? (Is it their unspoken case that there is no impact or is it their unspoken case that the students do not have a mind?) For how long does India plan to continue running its Scientific Establishment in English? What is the future of English in the rest of the World? What is the impact of an English-speaking Scientific Establishment on the Languages of India? What is the International Political impact of Indians speaking English? Do we have a position-paper on these critical questions on the interface of science and society? Do they realize that a large section of the World looks upon Indian Scientists as Monkeys–this word being having been explicitly used? If no, **they are not fit to be the Directors of Research Establishments or of Institutions of Higher Learning.**

India is a country that boasts about "respecting elders and Teachers" as part of our cultural heritage. India is a country that boasts about the "Guru-Sishya" relationship. Has any good quality teacher and/or any good quality student asked the question: "Is it morally right that the very respected teacher-student relationship functions in a language that is neither the teacher's nor the student's, nor the State's, nor determined by Scientific Procedure, nor by democratic procedure, but pushed on us by fraud? And then the **British Researchers themselves say – India has no thinking on the matter."**

Are then the Teacher-Student relations in this country not based on Fraud? So **there are no Teachers fit to be respected in this country, and there are no students fit to be taught in this country.** We suddenly determine that we cannot respect our teachers anymore? What about all the pledges we took? Have we forgotten them?

Should we quote here the conversation between Joseph Stalin and Vijaya Lakshmi Pandit, India's first ambassador to Russia when she presented her credentials to him:

Joseph Stalin: What is this Language?

Vijaya Lakshmi Pandit: "This is English"

Stalin: " I See — Is it your language?"

Vijaya Lakshmi Pandit:" Nooo.."

Stalin: "Well, if it is not your Language, is it my Language then?"

Vijaya Lakshmi Pandit: "NOOOO"

Stalin: "Are you not ashamed of yourself? You present me your credentials in a language that is neither yours nor mine?" ......"You are here to ask for my help. You come to me like a beggar and you talk to me in the language of the Pirates and Thugs?"....."Do you have no shame at all?"

NB: This ambassador could not meet Stalin again and had to leave Russia incomplete disgrace. (If you think that her treatment in English Speaking America –her subsequent posting– was any better, because she spoke English, we urge you to see for yourself, the discussions with Sam Rayburn. Stalin was more polite with the next ambassador, but asked him "What is your country doing about its Language problem?" The Ambassador replied "a committee is still working on it."

There is now a joke in Russia:

— *The Ambassador from India has come.*

–*We asked him "What is your language man?"*

–*He says that **he does not know what his language is…His Government is still trying to find out**.Until then he is going to speak to us in English !!!!*

CHAPTER EIGHT

Of Mathematicians, Nuclear Scientists & Drunken Disorderlies

About twenty years ago Chief Justice Krishna Iyer went to the Madras Club where he was invited to deliver a guest lecture. He went in traditional attire (for those who don't know, it is dhoti and shirt) and was told at the gate that he has to wear a suit because they had a dress code. The outraged Chief Justice aptly walked away from the venue without delivering a lecture, but made a pungent entry in the visitors notebook: *"My freedom as a citizen of India ended at the Gates of the Madras Club."*

Fast Forward to Chennai 2017: The prestigious Chennai Institute of Mathematical Sciences has openly declared on their website, albeit in more polite language, that the freedom for one and all who wish to visit the Institute will end at the footboard of the autorickshaw in Chennai. And just as Justice Krishna Iyer avoided the Madras Club, they are advising one and all to avoid the Chennai Autos. What?? The Most Brilliant Mathematicians of our country are being bullied by the autorickshaw drivers?

Shame on the Home Minister of Tamil Nadu and the Chennai's Commissioner of Police....who were willing to take care of the American Naval ships which docked in Chennai for re-fuelling. These American ships have been kicked out every other Asian country for their adulterous debauchery and for breaking down of all moral codes in dealing with Asian Women. **But this same Home Minister and Chennai Commissioner of Police cannot assure a safe travel to the Mathematicians of India or their guests when going to work in their own Chennai Institute of Mathematical Sciences?**

What a shame!

When a few girls coming from a midnight public Jazz program run by some foreign DJ scheduled in Bangalore were touched (no-doubt criminally by some goons, everyone shouted at the Bangalore Police as to why they could not provide security for a midnight event of a foreign jazz musician with alcohol being served. This was said to be an in-security for "Brand India". **But nobody shouted at the Chennai Police when our own Mathematicians are regularly bullied by a bunch of goons in broad daylight at the doorstep of their own Institute.**And thus, the Mathematicians of our country, to whom numbers are God, are confused on how to deal with their less fortunate brethren who merely to earn their own food, erroneously choose to Kick the God of the Mathematicians–the numbers?

In the past decade, there has been a spate of scientists working on issues linked either directly or indirectly to our defense, mysteriously dying in their own apartments, bathrooms or offices. Our press reported the conclusions on the cause of their death as ranging from their not being able to handle work-related stress, to their being homosexual. Coincidentally, these deaths occurred when India was forced to sign (bribed, blackmailed, threatened) the Civilian Nuclear Treaty, opening up India's nuclear programs for American/UN inspections. In most cases, these suicides (or murders?) occurred within the secured campus facilities. None protested or called for deeper investigation, including the victims' families. No public agencies investigated whether these suicides (or murders?) were related to threats forcing the Indian Scientific Establishment to surrender to the official line 'that the governments know and do what is best for their citizens' whereas governments, the world over, are cajoled, bribed and threatened to follow the objectives of international geopolitical players.

We have heard that India has made great strides in missile and Rocket technology, and sent missions to Mars–certainly no mean achievement. (As mentioned above, unless our nuclear-weapon is tested in missile-mated configuration, the intercontinental ballistic missile itself may not serve much purpose.)

But exactly while the press-titutes of the corporate-controlled-media used the artificially-created pro-Pakistan ruckus in JNU to divert our attention, our gold-mines have been auctioned away to foreign based companies on the basis of the claim that "India does not have the technology to mine gold".

Did no IAS officer, did no one in the HRD ministry ask the question: If we can send a mission to Mars, why can't we mine our own gold? If no, **they are not fit to be IAS officers** . Or is it their case **that money obtained by auctioning off the Indian National Gold Mines will be used to invest in real-estate on planet Mars?**(We are sure the IIM's of India teach their MBA students to make out such cases.)

Did the Vice-chancellor of the JNU where the ruckus was choreographed itself not ask this same question? No one is happy to hear that research funding sis being cut at JNU, but what were they doing? Clearly, the public ought to question the Vice Chancellor of JNU as to whether he was aware of this.

Did the Head the Dhanbad School of Mines (for example) or the Head of the Mining Engineering Departments anywhere else, or the Vice-Chancellors under which these institutions operate ask this same question? If no, **they better re-examine what is the duty of a good University's Vice-Chancellor.**

Did any HRD minister move to see to it that, in this configuration of things, IIT JEE rank number-1 should be counseled to go to Mining-engineering, and not Computer Science (the joke about Indian IT establishment having been already shown)? Presumably the HRD minister should have communicated this to the IIT's Directors who should have then passed this down to the entering-student counselors? **The HRD minister, the IIT Directors have then failed in their duty?**Let the entering students be guided by society running its own insane course? If you have no duty to your society, do you at least have a duty to your subject? **Is it the case that the sense of duty is badly disoriented by a malfunctioning society that treats these venerable figures as guides?** As suggested earlier, HRD more appropriately stands for Her-majesty's Re-usable Donkeys or Her-majesty's Recycled Donkeys (See section on Time_Travel to know more about the re-cycling process!!).

So, the Government has built a new IIT at Hyderabad? The Chief Minister of Andhra Pradesh, Rajasekhara Reddy died in a helicopter crash. The Black Box of this helicopter was sent to the NTSB in the USA for examination. The NTSB has extremely tight secrecy rules regarding the handling of the Black Boxes and it is not possible to get an independent picture once the Black Box is handed over to them.

Did even one responsible citizen of Hyderabad ask: "When we have IITs in India, why is the Black Box of our Late Chief Minister's crashed helicopter being sent to the US for reading...using the lame argument that the CBI does not have any aviation experts to analyze the Black Box. Can we or can't we read the Black Box recording in India itself? This will permit us to get a true picture of the death of our Chief Minister...other black boxes have been analyzed inside India." If no, **Hyderabad does not deserve an IIT.** Rather than building a new IIT at Hyderabad, **the correct thing to do may well be to understand and address the issues at the originally set-up IITs.**

To solve the dreadful water crisis that had started taking over several parts of India Government setup a grant of 10 crores, which was allocated to the then leading Dharwad University to find a solution for the drinking water crisis. The University came out with an excellent de-salination technology — Indian Scientists worked with Indian Money. But once this ingenious technology was discovered, the details were sold to Saudi Arabia for over 100-crores. **Saudi Arabia has used this technology to implement its water de-salination, but India has not till date implemented this technology discovered by our own scientists, which is anyway much less expensive than towing chunks of an arctic iceberg to the equatorial regions and getting the drinking water from there, as has been recently proposed!**

No PILs were filed for this wastage of public money, betrayal of trust in the critical area of providing Safe Drinking Water for all citizens of our country, nor was any investigation conducted to punish the guilty, now was there any suo-moto case in the matter. Instead, we have consolidated the position: "India's own Rivers and **Drinking Water for sale in India: by companies spawned from Pepsi and Coke, the same who have been kicked out of many small countries including Bolivia over a decade ago, for claiming to own all of Bolivia's water, including its rainwater!"**

A tremendous amount of distress was caused to the farmers when American Multi-National Giants pushed the BT cotton in India as a panacea for the production shortages of cotton, since the later years they raised the input costs to un-bearable levels. In Maharashtra and Gujarat alone, which is the cotton belt, there were 100,000 farmer suicides in Maharashtra only. Nationwide 250,000 farmers committed suicide — at an average rate of about 15-20,000 per year, or about 30 per day. The actual figures may be higher. After so many deaths, the Government awakened and asked the Ministry of Agriculture to come out with a local cheap variant for BT cotton seeds. After spending 2500 crores on this, they came out with a variety called SIRI as an alternative cheap variant for BT cotton.

But even after this the farmer-suicide rate did not recede. Further investigations revealed that after swindling away 2500 crores of Indian Government Money in the name of research, and having taken an equal amount from Monsanto, the leading Indian agricultural scientists have re-branded the Monsanto BT-cotton as SIRI and dumped it back on the Indian farmers causing further deaths with absolute impunity with no fear or sense of moral obligation. Finally the Government of India has to abandon the research and encourage the farmers to use native cotton seed varieties which are now doing very well in alleviating both financial and physical trauma the farmers are facing.

And now Monsanto and their corporate partners in India are once again trying to push the Government of India to force the farmers to abandon the native cotton varieties by selling GMOs as a panacea for the Indian problem. **The Agricultural Universities should be closed down , Scientists (Scientwists for the Multinationals) who are worse than Cannibals should be brought to criminal justice. No PILs filed, nor any suo-moto cases to take on this issue. No courts have looked into this matter, but Courts have time to shut down thousand year old cultural practices** like Jallikattu. Every political party in India has failed our farmers, who despite all odds hang on the land as their mother.

In all Western countries, every dam built on rivers is being blasted out to allow free flow of the rivers, as a response to the heavy damage to ecology and life and agriculture that is caused by the dams. The USA with 250,000 dams is blasting them out at a rate of about 1000 per year using the elite American Marine Engineering corps since the last 20 years.

Paradoxically, permission to build dams by Multinationals over Indian rivers is being given as if we are handing over candy to children — to the private corporations run by these Multinationals. Despite the Supreme Court's objection to this and despite knowing that water will be the future resource over which the wars will be fought, despite knowing that this process is causing a colossal damage to environments and to the very lives of our farmers, along with causing the privatized selling of water for perhaps first time in the history of mankind, especially in India.

In all the above cases, no PILs are filed, nor any suo-moto cases were taken by any of the courts in India, including the Apex court, who could wake up even in midnight hours and admit cases to ban spiritual and cultural practices in India coming from the past several thousands of years.

India has now a critical choice: **Is India meant to be sold as "Brand India"** – the brand being a midnight Jazz concert with a foreign DJ and intoxicated dancing public as seen in Bengaluru, concealing the terrible picture of farmers committing suicide on their parched lands and drying up rivers and of depressed and demotivated University faculty members most of whom are reduced to twiddling their fingers?? **Or Is India to be protected**, nurtured and strengthened **by guaranteeing the security of our scientists and by carefully guarding our Mathematical minds?**

CHAPTER NINE

Economists Or Fraudsters?

Around 1986 two professors, four readers and a few other management experts of the **"prestigious" IIM in Bengaluru have spent twenty or thirty crore rupees to finally determine after eight years that bullock carts are an indispensable medium of transport in India.**

But, until now none of those professors were able to figure out and explain to the people of India properly as to why when the USA, which has close to a 20-trillion dollar debt, its currency the dollar appreciates against the Indian Rupee — when we don't have any such level of debt? And why it is that without India having any such levels of debt why does the Indian rupee depreciates against the Euro or the Pound — that too when even for the forecasted recent economic debacle for post-Brexit Britain many Indian Businessmen have said that they will help to "Bail out Britain".

Despite having the ability to Bail out Post-Brexit Britain how is it that the Rupee Depreciates against the Pound, and despite post-Demonetization, close to 3-4 Trillion Dollars of Indian wealth, black money was converted into Dollars and Pounds, causing their demand to increase? Then why are we still borrowing money from the World Bank? And via FDI ? This has never been explained by any single Indian Leading/Non-Leading or Professional/Amateur Economist or Financial Experts.

Fortunately or unfortunately, even until today we do not have any calculation of the extent of the Black Money Generation in India, how it is stored and how it is transferred out of India to help every Western Economy....and then how this **same Indian Black Money is brought back to India as Foreign Direct Investment** ..to generate exorbitant interest? While Sec 2.4.9 of the Finance Ministry report suggests this last as a possibility, why does it stop at that? Why don't our investigative agencies push to calculate the certain amount? (**This will at least give the miserable IIMs some real numbers to work with, instead of consigning the poor blighters** to their bullock-carts!!)

But many leading Western Economic think tanks have already predicted correctly that the Annually Indian Black Money Generation is equivalent to its current White Money or GDP? Which means that India is the second largest economy, and not the fourth or fifth as many economists in India believe. If we add the black money generated in India over the past 25 years, since Liberalization, the total black money alone amounts to a whopping a minimum of 30-40 Trillion Dollars, enough to bail out American Debt, European Debt and the British Public and Private debt combined.

It is no wonder at all that suddenly every Western Nation wants to do business with India and get a share of this 40-Trillion dollar pie, which truly belongs to all the hard-working-honest-caring people of India, but is in the hands of a few commercial/political/ industrial/business houses and their lackeys and duly compliant bureaucrats. That is why every economist in India misrepresents this plunder and loot of India as Shining India or Developing India.

The very word Economics is a Greek Derivative whose literal meaning is "home-accounting". By extension, the country is considered as a home. Any simple, illiterate peasant, un-educated household-head will advise that you have to either live within the means of your income, or raise your income level to match your needs. And this simple peasant will also tell you that you cannot run a family on a constant state of borrowing. And if you cannot repay your debts, the money-lender will either take you to court and go behind your personal assets or will sell them to collect his debt and interest. And any householder will tell you savings for future calamities and maintaining a regular livelihood is the best strategy.

But irrespective of who ruled India, for the last 25 years from the beginning of Liberalization and Privatization, we have been encouraging exactly the opposite policies of "No savings at all", "absolute spending", "massive borrowing" and at the worst "encouraging people to invest in stock markets–which are equal to casinos –rather than in savings". No economist in India has raised a voice against this. Indians Economists want the country to adopt policies of the authorities blindly policies that they will not under any circumstances, implement at their family levels where they would always save money, buy properties, and never invest in gambling stock markets. So **why do these economists give approval when the government are doing something that is quite opposite to the** fundamentals of economic health, and something that is quite opposite of what they themselves do at home?Or does the word Economics mean to "play and gamble with other people's money"?

What a pathetic condition for the IIMs and on the other Economic departments in the country to be! The hard-working-honest people of our country had better decide to close down such fit-for-nothing, useless IIMs which do not give any convincing explanation and, more often than not, no explanation at all for what are directly observed phenomena?

However the IIM graduates and Economists of India may answer the above questions, the absolute irrelevance of the IIMs and of the so-called Economists in India and their pencil-eraser-sized brains, became glaringly clear during the recent saga of demonetization. Multi-million dollar paid economists and financial experts from any and every leading institute of India never satisfactorily explained to even the intelligent public as to how the re-introduction of the same currency after completely cancelling it out will prevent the further creation of black money that too when a new denomination of double the cancelled value is introduced, even if the cancelling may re-locate part of the currently existing black money. In fact, if you introduce a higher denomination currency which, in this case, was the 2000 rupee note, you are sending a public signal that you can actually double your black money in the next five years.

When we look at the first demonetization, India used to have currency values of 1000, 5000, 10,000 Rupees. When we demonetized the first time, the objective was to move this black money to Governmental control and use it for Nation-Building as opposed to it being used by petty private interests. To this end all denominations above 100 Rupees, were cancelled these denominations were not re-introduced for a long time — until India came under the regime of liberalization and privatization.

De-monetization as an economic measure has been implemented by several countries including as recently as Spain. However, in no case at all have any of these countries re-issued currency of a higher denomination or even the of the same denomination post the demonetization. Further-more, they have kept post-demonetization restrictions on withdrawals to a bare minimum, so that the newly printed currency, will immediately go back into circulation and get to work towards National re-building.

But strangely, for the first time ever in the entire history of money management, India re-introduced the same-denomination of currency what is even more surprising, introduced a higher-value denomination as well.

Somehow, contrary to all past-cases in the world, and contrary to all the laws of Economics as well as of Common Sense, it was somehow supposed to be "A War on Black Money". We did not hear any explanation that made any sense on this from any Economist anywhere in India. Minimal information that could be obtained in this regard was sketchy outlines by some public interest individuals on the Web.

In theory, the RBI could easily calculate the total number of notes printed since Independence, calculate the total value inside the Banking system, make a few subtractions (e.g. for soiled notes, forex etc) from the former and publish a "if-all-people-were-honest" estimate of the difference which should be the money outside the Banking system at the current point of time, thus giving some indication of the extent of the Black Money in the economy. While, this simple calculation would, by no means be any accurate measure of the amount of Black Money, it does not mean that this calculation should not be done, at least as a first analysis...somewhat like a "first-order-approximation" in scientific jargon.

What has been done, for example in a Finance Ministry Report on the subject is to start from complexity, then have various economists fighting with each other in the same report, so that even in the reports on Black Money published by the Finance Ministry itself, there are big differences in the estimates. So, therefore, it is left to the Public-at-large to do their best to understand what is happening around them.

Let us try to make an estimate of the amount of Black Money in India. A minimum limit can be determined on the Black-cash as follows:

The money deposited by General Public in this demonetization was ~14 Trillion Rupees (~0.25 Trillion USD). So at least these many notes are in circulation in this year; Assume 20% of the notes will be returned as soiled-notes (see IBGC report p53); recall the soiled-note-scandal brought to light e.g. by the Deve Gowda episode and known to have been in existence since the time of T.A.Pai, Mrs. Gandhi's advisor. These instead of being destroyed, are being returned to the Political Parties of whoever is in power. Over 40 years, this would be 56 Trillion Rupees, or about 0.9-Trillion USD, allowing wide for lower rates in the earlier part of the 40 years. This is the smallest of all numbers. For comparison, note that only one-fourth of it was returned by hard-working Indians in the current demonetization. (Bare-to-Bare minimum un-explained in this recent demonetization is 0.75 Trillion USD...Economists, please tell us what should have been the minimum deflation if 75% notes were properly and successfully annulled? What did public observe in this regard?...Even school-children can answer this question.)

The annual generation of Black Money in India as a fraction of the GDP; estimates on this one vary from 20 to at least 100%; the phrase Black Money and Black Economy perhaps being incorrectly used in each-other's place (related to each other by a velocity of money whose estimates again vary according to source, or no estimate at all for black-component) Based on this, the amount of Black Money generated since the first demonetization should be at a minimum 30-70 Trillion Dollars, allowing for very heavy variations as claimed in the Finance Ministry Report, and assumptions on the velocity as explained above.

The Black Money in the country can be also estimated from the Black Money outside using internationally available information and our assumption that only about 10% of the Country's Black Money will be moved outside (more on this 10% figure later).

The CBI report itself confirms over 500 billion USD is stacked by Indians in Black Money in Banks outside. This may be limited to the amount they have investigated, and is the very lowest of estimates, which will imply 5-Trillion USD black inside India. Just before the 2009 elections, Indian media reported that at least 1.4 Trillion USD is illegally held abroad. This is also the same estimate obtainable from a Global Financial Integrity report. From information on our first demonetization for every rupee came through banking system, 10 rupees was deposited by the religious institutions. So in current round, if USD250 billion entered into the banking channel, about 20 * 250 billion went via the Money Lenders – morphed religious institutions. This will give an estimate of USD 5 Trillion as the Black Currency. Next, we take the statement of our Current Prime Minister Honorable Shri Narendra Modi of the promise of bringing 15 Lakh Rs. into every Indian account from the Black Money abroad, this would present a figure of about 5-25 Trillion USD (assuming 1 account per 5- or per 1-person). German, Canadian and French reports say that about 7 Trillion USD belonging to Indians, with probably an equal amount in assets, is in the banking system outside India. So a figure of about 15 Trillion seems to be a reasonable figure for the amount of Black (cash+assets) stacked outside. According to the insider Herve Falciani who says the Government of India has taken only a miniscule amount of the data available with him, "millions of crores" are still flowing out. Even if you assume 'millions' means '5 millions' and the currency is rupees, this would tell us that about 1- Trillion

USD is flowing out. Although, he may not have used the word, if he implied 'annually' he most probably did. This figure of 1 Trilllion USD flowing out annually is also the estimate from GFI suggesting that in between 2002-6, the average outflow from all developing countries was 1 Trillion (referred to also in Finance Ministry report 2.7.4). India would have the major share. This would again indicate about 25 Trillion USD is some number for the Indian Black Money held outside, allowing for much lower values in the earlier years.

Thus, the total black cash inside the country may well be at a whopping 5-14-100-150-300 Trillion USD. The lowest being the CBI-accounts-investigated-confirmed figure, the high number stemming from the Falciani Calculation. The most reasonable one is 150 Trillion USD in black (cash + assets) inside India, since this is the figure stems from Honorable Prime Minister Narendra Modi as well as being the estimate of the Germans, the French, and the Canadians.

Recap: Black (Money + Assets) Estimates: Min: 5, Max: 500; Reasonable & Probable: 150 (in Trillion USD)

Please economists, money-managers, financial-wizards, RBI-heads, please answer for us, using even the lowest estimates above:

1)

If, not only the Economists of the country, but the Finance Ministry itself go on taking the position "this is impossible to estimate", "there are too many differing assumptions", "minimum available statistics-so-we-can't say", **then what is the use of any economic theory at all? Why don't the economic theorists close shop and go home?** Certainly at least now, if 86% of all the cash in the country were to be reset via the demonetization, using the highest technology we claim to have, then from now on these estimates should be re-doable to within 86% accuracy. **So, at least now, post de-monetization, do we have any fresh estimates of the Black Money in the country, or its rate of generation?** This would have been a very interesting study to do. Why haven't we seen it done?

2)

Do you have any reasonable studies on the Black-Cash to Black-Asset ratio? This ratio is critical in determining what will happen during de-monetization. **What explains the suggestion of a "leading" JNU Economics Professor, who is also called an "expert on Black Money", that this might be 1%,** recent tax raids are being used **to show this at 6%** (with no inputs on sample-size-details!!), when the figures from the 2012 **Finance**

Ministry reportof the Prosecuted Cases (Table 4.3, sec 4.7.12)- all the way from 2006-2012- **show this to be at about 50%, this last being the far more probable value?** (Strange that the JNU professor has also been quoted elsewhere in the Finance Ministry Report.) One wonders whether the "leading JNU professor, expert on black Money" has even bothered reading the finance ministry report. Would this be acceptable in any other Scientific field? Does his figure make sense when compared also against input from the IBGC (NIBM/Fletcher-CoC) report, which places a very high value on the M0 to M2 ratio in India—over 50%? It would appear that the figure 1% is the absolute upper limit for the Ratio **BrainUsed : BrainUnused** in India's educated elite.

3)

If you are not to able to estimate the "velocity" of the Black and the White components of the money, then how do you relate the Annual Black-Economy to Annual Black-Money Generation? What is your estimated error in the projection for these two figures? No mention whatsoever of this estimate is made in the Finance ministry report, **nor even is a value mentioned for the velocity.** Not only that, this report confuses Black Money, Black Income and Black Economy, starting off on the assumption that there is no accepted definition for these terms, then using one definition here, another there, and another from who knows where. (**How is this kind of a basic theoretical confusion seen in a Finance Ministry Report**—The report being signed off by our President?)

Request To all JEE-applicants, physics students and Scientists:

• **If the Director of ISRO were to sign off a report** prepared by ISRO scientists on the dynamics of its spaceflights, **using the terms "Mass", "Momentum" and "Energy"**(note our corresponding them with the economic terms above) **confusing them interchangeably according to whim and fancy, when the spacecraft is in accelerated curvilinear motion,** saying that these quantities "are vague and not definable" what would you have to say about this report? **Is the spacecraft flying according to scary-complicated equations in terms of immeasurable quantities that cannot be defined?** Will any science journal worth the name allow confused utilization of the terms **Entropy, Temperature and Internal Energy on the grounds that the Entropy is the indicator of disorder and cannot be estimated? Does any single professor of Physics in the country say that Entropy is a vague term and cannot be** defined?

- Why are the Economists allowed to get away with this? If none of these quantities are measurable or definable as they say, how do they calculate 1 dollar = 65.5 rupees and its change on a day-to-day basis so exactly?

4)

The ratio of Black (Cash+Assets) in India to The Same Amount Held Abroad is another critical number in determining what would happen during demonetization. Not only that this ratio is critical to understand many National-Security issues as well. **Do we have any estimate for this ratio?** Does the figure in the Finance Ministry's Report Annexure Table-1 **that the Swiss Banks** Liabilities towards **Indians is Rs 10,000 crores** (2010 figure, max 23k crore) make any sense if just one **low-level politician**in South India spent in the range of **Rs 500-1000 crores on his daughter's wedding post-demonetization?** Does this seem to compare with the claim "roughly 72.2 per cent of the illicit assets comprising the [Indian] underground economy is held abroad." as claimed by "The Drivers and Dynamics of Illicit Financial Flows from India" (pub: Global Financial Integrity) quoted by Sec 2.7.4 of Finance Ministry Report? **If these figures in the Finance Ministry Report have any credibility (which they don't as shown), does demonetization inside India make any sense at all, if 72% of the Black economy is outside India?**

5)

If the Government's Finance Ministry report itself is unable to estimate the annual Black Money generation to GDP ratio with standard deviations of over 100%, furthermore, confusing the Black-Economy with the Black Money Creation, then **how do they project a deflation-calculation if the Black Money were to be properly, as they claim, annulled?**And have they made this projection at all?

6)

To all High-School students: What should have been the expected deflation if there was 0.25 Trillion USD in white, and 4.75 Trillion USD Black, if the Black Money was truly and properly annulled? Did we observe anything even remotely close to this? Please repeat this calculation using not the bare-minimum, but using instead the Prime-Minister's indication on the quantum of the Black Money. What would be the deflation figure in this case? This is a question even a school-child can answer. Even if you make the ridiculous assumption of BMOutisdeIndia:BMInsideIndia = 72:28

still what does this deflation work out to?

7)

If this was **not the observed deflation** in the society, then:-

8)

What happened to the Black Money, if it was not somehow re-introduced into the system?

9)

Was it the case that the Black Money was transferred outside the country, and is being re-introduced into the system according to the aims and convenience of the foreign geopolitical players, thus prevent the Indian public from realizing the much lower inflation rate that would have been expected? (as we shall see below this may be the only consistent alternative)

10)

At what speed was the **Black Money re-introduced back** into the system?

11)

What would have been the impact of the withdrawal restrictions and the supposedly-slow-printing rate on the Velocity of a) the white money b) the Black component? If as the public saw, the Black Money was given out in thousands of crores without restrictions at all, while white-moneyed people stood in line for 4000Rs, would this not result in a much-much higher Black-Money-Velocity than the White Money-Velocity? **Thus increasing the Black-Economy several fold?**

12)

Would the Velocity of the Money change after demonetization? Did you make any estimate of the change? "RBI working paper series 06 31 May 2011" has made predictions on the velocity of the M3-money over various time-span of decades with quarterly variations (this value being now very low, near 1.3). So we would have expected to see this for example in the RBI report on demonetization dated 10 March 2017. We do not see any such forecast. Nor did we see a single Indian media-article using this figure. (The RBI report does however indicates that the M3 component was stable except for a 2-month pre-demonetization high. If the M3 component is stable, but the in this context, the value for M0 figure is more critical, but this figure has not been published. Note also from the graphs in "RBI working paper series 06 31 May 2011" that velocities of M1 and M2 components react differently to the M1 and M2 components themselves.

Note also the IBGC (NIBM/Fletcher) report on the very high role of the M0 component in India compared to that of other countries. Note also for example and as expected, that the paper "Velocity of Money Function for India.." shows clearly that the velocity of the narrow money has stayed consistently high over decades, while the velocity of the M-3 component has fallen significantly.) The obvious question that ought to come to the public mind is: If a much higher currency of 2000 rupee note was introduced post-demonetization, and if there was no change in the velocity of money, and with assumptions made on the unavailable M0 value, what would be the impact on the Black Economy, given that the Black Economy is related to the Black Currency via the velocity of money? Wouldn't it then be set to increase?

13)

If the much-smaller white money component itself took several months to print as the government claims, and if this massive Black-Money component was some-how re-introduced into the system before we could even see the common-sense-expected figure for the deflation, **how was this miraculous Currency Printing Technology achieved? Was it achieved in India?**Or was it outsourced? The answer to this last question is well known. Money printing has been outsourced to companies in the US, UK and Germany; while the issue has been mentioned in the Parliament, no discussion on the implications of this is seen by Indian Security Analysts anywhere.

14)

The RBI has refused to answer questions posed under the RTI, clearly stating that there would be a "threat to life" if they answered. Whose responsibility is it to ensure their security? Either the RBI's economists have completely failed in their duty to the People of India, ORIndia's Internal Security Apparatus has failed to provide them the Security and allow them to speak the truth. Either way a change in the country's way of functioning is required. In section -11, we shall discuss this issue of the "threat-to-life" in more detail.

That none of these questions can be answered and no numbers are given in itself is the proof that the De-monetization is not what it was stated to be, AND it is also proof that the IIMs, the Economic Professors, Financial Experts of the country have badly failed in their duty, relying on big words rather than on solid calculations and theory. If it a question of lack of knowledge or of ignorance in the Economics and finance departments, they better get to some serious studies because they are using Public Money and getting Public Respect. Why have they not done it upto now? But, more seriously, if they have the knowledge and do not want to do this calculation, either out of fear or for selfish cause, then they are certainly complicit with the Fraud and Economic Crimes Perpetuated against the people of India, and are Seditious. **We suggest they close shop and go home.**

P.S. A polite note to the Physical Scientists and Mathematicians of India

"Laymen Cannot Understand Economics" –is that what we are told? **When Physicists can show without any doubt** to anyone who sits with them the calculation of the Avogadro Constant at 6.022141086 * 10 exp 23 (mol-inv), or the Boltzmann Constant at 1.38064852 * 10 exp -23 (MKS)–- **these Indian economists have the crass ill-mannered impertinence to tell our students or anyone from other departments who questions** them that they can't show to "laymen" the calculation of the Dollar-Rupee Exchange Rate at Rs 67.5, starting with the simple Fischer exchange rate theory, nor can they show the calculation for the rapid rate of change of this exchange-rate which has occurred several times in the past.

Scientists have a duty to their country...when numerical fraud is occurring it is your duty to shout.............. whether it is in your department or not.......Otherwise the theoretical **Astrophysicist, who ponders and writes equations governing the deep meaning of the Universe, is no better than the rude Governmental Clerk who when approached for help at his desk says: "Nikal Jao! Yeh Mera Kaam Nahi Hai, Mai Kuch Nahi Jaanta Hoon."**

Scientists from the other fields have a duty to tell the whole country that the more likely reason these economics professors "could not show the calculations to laymen" was that there was a fraud of un-imaginable proportions played out here, and that either the Brains of the IIM's MBAs and of the Economists were stupefied, or that they were in collusion....most probably a combination of both.

No other group in the country has the ability and fearlessness to plunge into theories and equations as do the Physicists. Everyone else in the country is afraid of theories and equations, which are being used to trick them. You are the only ones who can catch these propagators of chicanery, cheats and tricksters out.

If any self-righteous economist tries asking "You are a layman. Can you understand the term 'velocity of money'? ". **HIT BACK AT THESE**

MONKEYS and don't be afraid to ask them why it is called "velocity" when there is no associated direction. If the Physicists were to understand the answer to this question they would have understood a key element of how the fraud is played out. Starting from here, expose them one lie at a time...one stupidity at a time..one fraudulent equation at a time. **Let us remind Indian Scientists of other Departments that it is their duty to SHOUT at these economists-fraudsters!!**

Once again, let us remind particularly the physicists of one of their pet subjects: "The Theory of Relativity" from which basis the Mass-Energy Equivalence stems, the latter having being the critical element of the nuclear-energy release which has devastated Japan. Let us tell them that therefore while the "Theory of Relativity" could in good sense be called the basis of the destruction of Japan's Hiroshima and Nagasaki, **India is being destroyed not by Relativity but by what is called "Relativism"**...something that you may have contemptuously said is the work of "useless Philosophers who play with words", but can't write a single equation.

Let also the Physicists of India take note, that it is the same power lobby that uses both Relativity and Relativism. **The lobby that pushed Relativism into India,** earlier primarily via the "Advaita Ashrams" (but now we are already destroyed by it) is the **same lobby that pushed the hand of President Truman to drop the bomb on Japan,** despite democratic America's overwhelming public opposition to this move; and it is the **same lobby that has pushed this nonsensical term "velocity of money"** into economic theory.

If you don't take some time to step out of the world of Physics to understand this process and challenge this fraud, you are failing in your duty to your society, what is more you may well be un-wittingly perpetuating the destruction of your own society. **You alone are capable of helping India now to resolve the mess we are in.**

What a tragic twist of fate for a country which claims to have given the Artha-Shastra to the world —this same Artha-Shastra was and being is duly followed to the letter in every Western Country, including in Pakistan, and yet waiting to be utilized for the betterment of the Indian economics.

Now let us look at the current demonetization.

CHAPTER TEN

From Indian Economic Miracle To Anglo-American Economic Miracle

What we call the Indian Economic Miracle is nothing but the sweat and blood of millions of Indians from the day we got independence, in whatever fractured way, and were left to the vultures of international banking and financial elite. The new nation thus born was left with less than Rs 100 crores to manage, survive and grow. Immediately thereafter, a horrific war and partition was pushed upon us, which saw assets worth close to a trillion USD being wiped out. After this 1-Trillion dollar loss, and before we could recover from the human and resource loss of partition, Mahatma Gandhi was assassinated and the country was thrown into a psychological trauma and a now mental partition was further created:- a permanent division of "Secularists" versus "Nationalists", where both these groups being actively created and controlled by the British as part of their divide-and-rule strategy. It is indeed a remarkable feat by the political-religious community and social leaders to put this trauma of the Mahatma Gandhi's death on the back-burner, and yet with a heavy heart and with a single mind dedicated to re-build the nation to the level of a world-power in the next five years.

In this situation, the visionary Indians and leaders and people came together as a family to embark on re-building our Nation, with a sheer determination to survive and reclaim the ancient glory of India, with whatever little knowledge that was left over with them post the manipulations of the British.

These Visionaries adopted a socialist economic model for infrastructure development and an agrarian economic model for the food-self-sufficiency and embarked upon massive public sector investments to achieve self-sufficiency in defense. But still continuing the British-trend, Banking, Insurance and Oil industries were left in the Private hands, and these perpetuated frauds and prevented the formation of Capital in India.

With a single master stroke, Feroze Gandhi nationalized all the insurance industries, resulting in the now gigantic LIC. The money needed for development of infrastructural projects was thus the people's savings put into the LIC. The war with China was slapped onto us, with two aims: to de-moralize our army and secondly to drain our economic resources. Nevertheless, millions of unfazed Indians donated whatever they wore in Gold towards financing the defense of our country in this war. After the war with China, we nationalized our Banking and after the 1971 war India nationalized the oil industry, and expanded our Public Sector Units to cover many more fields in our life.

Without a single rupee by way of foreign debt, India generated Lakhs of Crores internally to achieve remarkable food- defense- and economic-sufficiency. And when the internal security apparatus realized that the British agents in India whose properties were nationalized became the conduits for the creation of the Black-Economy and the Black-Money on a massive scale, with the stroke of pen most of that Black-Money was neutralized and brought into the Public Accounting domain for further development of India making it a leading nation in terms of Science, Space and Nuclear Energy.

We mention again that in the previous round of demonetization, higher-denomination currencies that were cancelled were not re-introduced. This toil of the sweat and blood of the poor, common, honest Indian with the vision, and iron-willed dedication and patriotism towards the country and a colossal understanding of the geopolitical and international colonial dimensions of death and destruction, though not exactly termed as geopolitics, made India by the turn of the century a giant economic engine based on its own strength of manufacturing and agriculture with a USD 1.2 Trillion white and USD 1.2 Trillion black economy (pre-Liberalization).

But around the world, by this time, the so-called Anglo-American Economies were collapsing under the massive burdens of debt, which they had incurred by complicated webs of fraud and colossal greed and hedonistic avarice. That is where their strategists realized that they could survive if they could parasite on the Indian Economic Miracle, and by plundering what the hard working Indians had created over the past 60 years. This was done by privatization and Liberalization, with the Privatization being spear-headed by the erstwhile owners of the East India Company i.e. the Bank of England. In doing so, they also fulfilled the promise made by Mountbatten to Churchill: "if Churchill were to lend unconditional support to his India-independence theory for now, in the next 50 years, not just British India, but the entire India would be re-occupied." Perhaps, this may the only instance where an Englishman has kept his word.

Towards the middle of the twentieth century, the Colonial Era started winding down, and socialist republics started coming up. All newly formed republics and nation-states have realized the only way to re-build and recover their economies after the plunder perpetuated during the colonial era was to follow the economic model of socialism, with the government spending left over economic resources for the benefit of one and all. Thus starting from 1920 to 1970, huge economic assets were created in more than forty or so countries under the tight control and supervision of their own watchful governments. Though there were complaints about some level of mismanagement of the funds, but on an overall level, trillions of dollars worth of economic assets were created in these countries, these assets being off-limits to every Colonial Power.

In the absence of the free flow of goods under the concept of global free trade, the colonial powers started starving and could not even enter the economic structure, with the exception of the USA which had cornered most of the reparations from World War -2. Thus, the push started from 1950's to disrupt these socialist economies and oust their political leadership under any available flimsy pretext, and to install puppet regimes which would then sell off the massive economic assets of the country under consideration for a few cents or for a dollar.

Every war that happened during this period, every coup that took place aimed at knocking down the socialist republics one after the other and sucking their economic resources into the un-maintainable, wasteful Western Economic Lifestyle based on faulty economic theories. After thirty such countries were knocked down, the process of divide and rule and plunder was christened with a nice-sounding name: "Privatization and Liberalization". The theoretical framework of this was proposed by the Chairman of the Bank of England around 1971. The final frontiers in this process of knocking down the country's economic resources were Russia and India.

Russia with an estimated worth of 75 Trillion USD natural economic resources became the prime target during the eighties. The Colonial Powers almost succeeded in occupying Russia, but for the dawning of the era of Vladimir Putin who ruthlessly purged one and all, literally hunting them whether inside or outside the country, and restoring the economic self-reliance of Mother Russia. With Russia slipping out of their hands, the eyes were set on an unfathomably resource-rich country, which even after thousand years of non-stop plunder and looting still captures the imagination of one and all, thugs, thieves and robber-barons alike with her yet-unknown massive resource potential — that country is India.

With the assassination of two Prime Ministers in succession, a stage was set for the final round of Liberalization and Privatization in India, using the Mantra of "Development" as if India was some aboriginal country.

The Black component inside India, in terms of assets and cash alone is more than 70 Trillion USD. This is roughly equal to the value of the entire natural resource base of Russia. No one knows how much Gold is with the people, no one knows how many diamonds, precious stones and metals are with the people and religious and spiritual institutes of India, no one knows how vast the unexcavated Gold Reserves. No one knows what quantity of other natural economic resources including the rare-earth metals are hidden within the Indian continent, no one knows what were the technologies used to extract and use them over the past thousands of years.

But what certainly they knew are the following facts and statistics that were compiled over the past fifty years since Independence, though we have a phenomenal, abysmal ignorance about what India had in terms of human and economic resources prior to Independence. The value of immovable property of the several-thousand or so spiritual and religious institutions of Karnataka alone is valued at 30-50,000 crores (7.5 b USD). The most conservative estimate of the Gold holdings under one vault alone of the temple of Shri Padmanabha Swamy in Tiruvanathapuram is valued at a whopping Trillion USD. The income generated from the former united Andhra-Pradesh state from the Prostitution rings alone is in far excess of Rs 30,000 crores (4.5 b USD) per year. (Rs 1000 crore ~ 155 million USD)

The register maintained in the Tirumala Temple that deals with the broken non-usable discarded jewellry is more than 500-billion USD. The average wealth amassed by any Chief Minister who held the position for more than a decade is over 50,000 crores (7.5 b USD). The total amount of money swindled away in the top 35 scams is over 8 Lakh crore (120 billion USD). The amount of NPAs written off by the SBI recently is 280,000 crores (42 b USD). The total amount of tax evaded by major 30 industrial corporations over the past fifty years is close to 3 Lakh crores (45 b USD). It is no wonder these figures with large numbers of zeroes do not make sense to Indians, but they make very clear economic sense to the collapsing Western Economies, who realize that India can bail out every other economy of the World for the next 100 years. The list if we start compiling about what we have, what we are losing, will be a Magnum Opus of two or three volumes and could well be titled "Corrupt Indians".

The Indian economy now stands at 1.2 Trillion USD, which is what we call the white economy and the Black economy is another 1.2 Trillion USD. Our entire national debt is less than 90 billion USD.

If the massive assets created under the Indian Economic Miracle were to be sucked out of India, this would create a massive Western Economic Miracle. This process has started since 1985 and is continuing with and incremental numbing and dumbfounding of the minds of the Indian population, subjecting them to a massive array of propaganda with every Government turning India into a sloganocracy rather than into a thinking participative democracy.

The current round of demonetization is the first large-scale plunder executed on India. Let us take a closer look. On the surface, we invalidated all the 500 and 100 Rupee notes and in the process, according to official figures, 14 Trillion Rs (~0.25 billion USD) moved into the Banking system, from the general working public. Then we re-introduced the same denomination 500 and a double denomination of 2000; the last two steps having no precedent in the entire history of demonetization the world over.

And then, we clamped restrictions on withdrawals to the bear-minimum limits, thus cornering all the cash into the Banking system. What happens to the velocity of the white money here? It drops heavily. High school students can predict its impact on the Economy.

Of particular note is that this 14 Trillion Rupees (0.25 Trillion USD) was the money put into the system by the General Honest and Hard-working people of India, the vast majority of who are not black-money hoarders. The black money which is about several tens of times this amount which was stacked up with the corrupt officials, politicians, industrialists, hawala dealers and other such groups, could not and did not go into the Banking system, if it did there is an obvious problem. Then where did it go?

Enter the Re-monetization of Black Money. Where did the massive amount of Black Money go? It is a simple question to which everyone knew the answer....even a rickshaw puller on the street could tell you the first part of where the black money went. But amazingly neither the corporate media, which has become a mirror image of the US fake media, nor the Indian economists, nor the Indian bankers ever discussed this question, the first part of the answer to which being common knowledge in the public.

But anyway, the following lines will explain de-monetization. Most of the money that has not entered the system from the above groups, valued at a barest of minimum estimates at 5 Trillion USD was bought by many illegitimate money-exchangers at a discounted-rate, up-to 40%. These money exchangers who are connected to various political parties who were financing gold-, dollar-, pound- and diamond- and narcotic-smuggling operations and are spread all across the West Coast, Delhi and Southern Coastal towns of Tamil Nadu and Kerala, swung into action and purchased the entire Black Money at a discount of 40%. The next obvious question is does, either the Enforcement Directorate, the Income Tax Department, the CBI, the Police, the IB or any other branch of the Government have a detailed list of who these illegitimate money-exchangers were?

Now the next obvious question is why did these illegitimate money-exchangers do with if this invalidated currency has no value? Were they Saints trying to help the people of India who could not go to the banking system for help?

Well no, the same people who violate every international and national law and became a vehicle to suck the blood of the Indian Common Man could not have suddenly become saints! They did not purchase the money to alleviate the suffering of their fellow Indians at 40% discount. Then, what did they do with the cash?

Someone pointed a finger blaming the Banks. So, we had to believe that when the common man was standing for hours in the heat of the Sun to withdraw 4000 Rupees, that the "Corrupt Bankers" sold all the newly printed currency of the same-denomination to these black-money hoarding groups in high priority order (e.g. in just one exposed case, a low-level party official was caught with several thousand crores of newly issued currency). First of all, they became richer overnight by about 30%, and this entire money now being legitimate. And what did they do with the new money?

This legitimized money was then transferred out of India into the US, Cananda, England and Israel by purchasing dollars, pounds, diamonds and gold in the international markets. **This sudden flow of money into the International Markets from India explains overnight hike in the price of Gold, and the hike in the exchange value of dollar and pound,** though there was no valid economic reason that existed either in Europe or in America at that same time to explain this hike. So when **every leading European economist had predicted that the value of the Pound will fall heavily** post-Brexit, but yet —defying all those predictions of the European Economists— yet lo and behold! Surprise of surprises !! —**the pound actually appreciated and Britain declared that they would be able to sustain the economic losses of the Brexit.** At the same stretch of time, **even US and Canada predicted a revival of their nearly-destroyed real-estate markets** and a revival of their long-pending infrastructure projects slated **at a whopping 2-Trillion USD?**

So, then from the Perspective of the Americans and the British, the obvious question they asked for their own motive was: **"Why not ?? — Why not let Britain Survive and Why not let America Revive?"** To accomplish this, both of them were able to move 4 Trillion USD of hard earned money Indian money into their economies, from India and pump it into their economies in a matter of one week.

No wonder then, the Head of State of the British Government and of the erstwhile British East India Company was present in India, perhaps symbolically, to ensure that the money was properly transferred to them during the period of de-monetization; and no wonder all of this gang of Money Lenders praised her and elevated her to the level of Durga, so that she could punish the fingerprintable-biometrically-tagged-thieves and slaves of India one more time and can loot their wealth away.

While our own Prime Minister Mrs Indira Gandhi was not allowed entry into the Puri temple on the flimsy grounds that she had married a Parsi (who are actually very much a part of our own civilization), the British Prime Minister, a foreigner and of a semitic faith was by your own priests elevated to the level of the Goddess inside the sanctum sanctorum of a Temple, precisely when this saga was going on.

No wonder also then that the Israeli president was present in India at this same time, to smoothen the workings of the transfer of the trillions of dollars and pounds. This entire saga being too complex for the so-called Indian Economists to understand, our Prime Minister decided not to rely on them and handed over the process of de-monetization to Israeli-based economists and their advisors, and himself set out for a vacation in Japan.

Does this explain why our Honorable Prime Minister **did not take the advice of Indian Economists, but chose to depend instead upon Israeli Economists**/American Economic Think Tanks/British Based Friends-and-Family **for his de-monetization decision?** Every other country that de-monetized including as recently as Spain, never re-issued the same denomination or a higher denomination currency after demonetization. In fact, after demonetization, these countries have kept a restriction on withdrawals to a minimum limit, so that whatever is currently printed to the extent of cancelled denomination, it is used for the National rebuilding.

On a relatively much smaller note, let us mention what was done with the money deposited in the banks. Once the money was collected into the Public Sector Banks and put the restrictions on the cash withdrawals, they have written off the No-Performing-Assets bad loans to the tune of lakhs of crores, which were in the first place, given to the Politicians or Industrialists who have borrowed thousands of crores and never paid back a single penny (e.g. Kingfisher, Tata and many others) across the political spectrum under every government since Liberalization. Most of this money was used to revive sick industries in Britain, Europe, America, from which not a single pie was paid back to the Indian Banks. By cancelling all this debt, we have converted Indian white money into that much black money in the economy..... the Black money problem has actually worsened.

The wise bankers have not yet explained why a common man could not withdraw more than 4000 Rs from an ATM while politically connected Industrialists could withdraw thousands of crores and invest this England and America to revive their sick Industries. Of course, the Banking Chiefs are saying they are not cancelling the loans, but are keeping them in the Escrow Accounts and will collect them later. Somebody should explain to the people of India that if in the last 60 years they could not collect a single pie from them, there is no chance whatsoever of them doing it now.

In order to facilitate the help given by these Bankers and government, the unscrupulous politicians/industrialists, the requirement to put the identities of the donors on the political contributions has been removed in the recent finance bill.

But the banks are not only sitting on Rs 2.85 Lakh Crores (60 billion USD) of NPAs, they are also sitting on 100 times that value in terms of physical assets, which according to accounting depreciation rules will show as zero in their books. But the experienced accountants, international bankers, crooked politicians and the heirs of the East India Company, know the value of these assets and of the banks that own them. And Governments want to privatize these Public Sector Banks for all this "India-loving, India-favoring, India-Development" shouting groups do not want to purchase these PSUs with the debt. So they want to zero out the debt, purchase the bank suck the invisible assets and exit. So much for the domestic aspect of what was done with the white money collected. It was converted into Black Money, although the scale was much smaller than what was done with the money outside India.

But there is still something does not add up with the picture presented above. If the Indian banks had got 14 trillion rupees this gets only 200 billion dollars. But the cash infusion into the American and British economies as explained above was about 4 Trillion Dollars. Then where did the balance come from? As has been noted even in our Parliamentary Committee Reports, the printing of Indian currency has been given to more than one foreign country more than once before. The public of India learnt about it much later via the Parliamentary reports. It would of course now merit the question: **So, in the recent de-monetization (both prior to- and post-) was the money printed from outside the country and the figures being given to us by our financial centers the correct ones cannot be taken for granted?**

The complete absence of any critical role of our own Economists and of our own IIMs and the minimal role if any of the NIBM, in what is a major national economic process, is indicative of their actual irrelevance in anything meaningful or in anything that is directly observed. Neither did we see them as much as offer the above explanation or any other convincing explanation to the people of India who experienced the event, nor were they taken into confidence by their own government.

Why can't we see an independently-set up panel of Eminent Economic Professors being given an insight into the working of the RBI and be able to come up with Economic Theories that will tell us what is really happening in the country? This panel changing every two-years or so and drawn up from Universities across the country? Instead of the public seeing a highly erratic set of facts, confused theories combined with big words being used to destroy all common-sense questioning, with Economic Professors giving explanations that are only marginally more illumining than that which un-educated common men talk, aping the words put into their ears by the corporate fake media?

But in the absence of this valid scientific process, the public are being left with no choice but to to start dis-believing their own financial authorities.

CHAPTER ELEVEN

Gold Wars: From Demonetization To DeAurization

It is time to look at the question of the "threat to life" argument cited by the RBI when questions were posed to it under the RTI act. While this did find mention in a few newspapers, the Indian public at large are guilty of not following up this matter with the appropriate questions. We urge the gullible members of the Indian public to realize the seriousness of the "threat to life" of the RBI core team, we please urge the Bank Staff push for increased security as well to please take necessary steps to increase awareness among themselves and the Indian public for example about the **assassination of the Germany's Deutsch Bank Chief — Alfred HerrHausen — because he wanted to write off loans to the developing countries**...just contrast this with our Banks writing off loans given to the puppets of the Multinationals...the same group which assassinated HerrHausen. **Strange it is (or not!) that No Indian media ever spoke about the Alfred HerrHausen assassination in this context**...the corporate fake media...why would it?? We urge citizens of India to realize that **the forces that assassinated Alfred HerrHausen are precisely the same forces that are threatening the RBI** and causing them to say "threat-to-life" to turn down RTI queries. It is the duty of every responsible Indian to ask whether the **life of our Prime Minister has also been threatened by these same forces.** Do recall his statements carefully. We urge you to stand by your Prime Minister and pull India correctly out of the situation, rather than fight amongst yourselves whether de-monetization was good or bad. It does not speak well of Opposition Party members who started shouting "Mr. Prime Minister! Please tell us who is trying to kill you!". It is the duty of the opposition parties to explain these forces to the people, rather than to fight with the Prime Minister. If Indians do not spend time to study and understand these forces, they will forever be blaming the Pakistanis for everything that is happening under the Sun.

The army's duty may perhaps be to defend borders and to protect the nation from external threat. But, what they should be defending is not an imaginary line drawn by the British, but rather a geographical entity in given time and space. This entity is not a barren piece of earth—it is full of people and resources. As they do when internal calamities such as floods, earthquakes, riots strike — so too, it is their paramount duty that when people in high power and responsibility express a "threat to their lives" while duly discharging their responsibilities under the constitution, the army should work in tandem with the Internal Intelligence agencies and neutralize the threat originating and manifesting either internally or externally.

The fact that this has not been reflected in the current situation indicates the lack of understanding of external threat to the republic, and how this threat is manifesting within the borders of India.

Indians ought to take some time off to salute the courage of The German Deutsch Bank Chairman, who was assassinated for reminding the world of the responsibility of the Colonial and neo-Colonial money monsters to forgive the debt of many third world nations as it was the third world that was completely exploited by the same forces, and it was actually their own money, that was plundered during the colonial era, being lent to them.

Sadly, if we contrast this with the Indian context, though several members of our country's highest offices, starting from our own Prime Minister to RBI's chief employees, expressing the same threats on their lives, the country did not make any assurance to protect them. In the absence of such assurances to protect them, out of fear for their own lives, they have chosen the path of their own survival and implemented policies that were far more destructive for India rather than those implemented by the EICs themselves. Of course, here we can see the very clear influence of the Western Education on the Indian mind, especially in the interpretation of Darwinian theories of survival of the fittest ... not survival of the strongest. In this process, where the fittest try to survive, as a result of ensuring survival of the People in Authority by the People in Authority and by the Political Power, the most ancient the strongest, the most vibrant, Universal Scion i.e. India is being slowly bled to death.

Though there are many in India who are seeing the inevitable death, part following part, it is time for we the people of India to wake up and avert this death and bring India back to life and Vibrancy both as a leader of the Non-Aligned-Movement and as the Universal Beacon of Light to uplift the suffering of humanity.

So the de-monetization happened anyway, as mentioned above the highest leadership in our national institutions were threatened with their lives and made the easier choice. Some discussion was provided in the earlier sections.

All very good, but if we look carefully, we see that the **British-based forces that organized this,** could have easily achieved their goals **without the de-monetization. If the currency can be easily printed outside as has been done in the past, and has without any shadow of doubt is being done now,** and will be done in the future too, the foreign-exchanging of USD 4Trillion could have been done without the de-monetization. Even if they wanted to remove USD 4 Trillion from India, there were many other ways they could have done it. **So, why then go for the de-monetization at all?** The answer lies in understanding that both the UID's Aadhaar Project and the recent de-monetization are a test-run.

More precisely, **they are the test-run using psychological warfare to see how the Indian citizens react to absurd, illogical, humiliating decisions pushed on them via sloganeering**. As has been stated earlier, in order to loot the complete wealth out of India, a critical step is to numb the minds of the population at large.hey wish to see whether the Indian citizens who have been softened and pampered with the comforts of Liberalization and Privatization will choose to keep asking for the toffees and keep accepting increasing levels of humiliation or whether they will be able pull their gaze away from the toffee, to see the picture correctly and stand for what is right, as opposed to begging for what is pleasant.

This information on how the Indian public will react to absurd, illogical orders coming ostensibly from their own Government is necessary for the foreign-planners to determine the next strike. Here we shall restrict ourselves to outlining only **one dimension of this next strike.**

According to leading World Economic Bodies,there is about 160,000 tons of gold mined in the world over the last 200 years. Out of this, close to 120,000 tons are with the European Union, the Bank of England, and with the USA. This will then leave 40,000 tons with rest of countries. This figures representing the gold mined across the world over last 200 years.

At the current value 1 ton = 30 million USD, this gold would be valued at about 5 Trillion USD. Large though this figure seems, it is not comparable to the World's GDP, in fact as seen above, it is only equal to the absolutely-low-end estimate for the Black Cash that may be in India. So, then what is the point in shouting Gold-Gold-Gold? In fact, if this were the case, then the Gold value should have been much higher than it is today, about a 100 times higher.

To answer this question again, we look at India. From the internationally-available figures, of the 650 tons of gold produced annually, 80 % flows into Asian Markets. Of this 80%, 70% flows into India. This has been the case since Independence. This will put an estimate of 15,000 tons as the minimum amount of Gold imported into India post-Independence, worth about 500 billion USD. No big deal here. But there is something else that we should look at. **That is the question of the amount of Gold that existed in India pre-Independence. This figure will turn out to have meaning and strategic importance.** Let us estimate below.

Let us look at just one simple example. When the Kingdom of Amravati fell to the British, it was then looted. At the time the Capital of that small tiny Kingdom, all houses and Palaces were gold plated. The British cavalry used 7000 horses to carry away the loot from the City. But we never read about this our History books. We learn about this from the records kept in Telugu, as well as from records kept by the French sources. What the British have done is **to cut-paste this same story onto Ghazni — that he looted Somnath, and carried away its gold on 7000 horses.** Chor! Chor!..Udhar ....Udhar Dekhiye Sharmaji.....Vahaa Jaa Ra Hai Chor.

Another simple Example: when the grandchildren of a mere clerk in the East India Company in today's England were running short of pocket money, they merely opened one of the thousands of warehouses containing the loot of the East India Company, and took out just six small items. These few items were put on auction in the famous London Christies and fetched 5 million pounds. This, we may add, was splashed across every major Indian news media with great pomp. So, what must have been the total size of the warehouse and what figure would we arrive at if we added the figures for the unknown thousands of such warehouses that hold the 100-yr loot by EIC sailors, clerks, officers, Lords, Governor Generals who worked in India. That will give a base-point of how much money that was looted from India. Yet, it will not tell you how much money that was there in India. And, when they did not find anything in India, those few unlucky individuals of the EIC picked up every any articraft from ancient temples, main deity idols, manuscript, mathematical texts, astronomical texts, medical texts, metallurgy texts whatever was available, in whichever language it was available was taken out and fortunately, they were able to make millions of pounds, by auctioning these texts again in London's Christie Auction House and other Auction houses set up there.

Most of these auctioned items were purchased and preserved by the Germans and French, who at the time felt that the British were destroying the cultural scientific heritage and the beacon of the civilizational progress that was India. Post WW-2, some of these articrafts were taken by the Russians who preserved them as well. No spiritual or religious leader in India has any clue of the extent of what was lost from their spiritual and religious organization. By the way, one such object which was carefully lifted from the Kashmiri Temples that was auctioned and purchased by the Germans and preserved in Germany was given to our Current Prime Minister, when he visited Germany.

Were not the Germans expecting a few questions from us, when they told us that the idol belonged to a Kashmiri temple, from the era of Emperor Lalitaditya? If they were, they would have been badly disappointed. We were happy with the gift and we sent a message to German Chancellor thanking her for the gift. But surprisingly none neither historians nor spiritual leaders nor nationalists etc. bother to ask even a single question. If, according to the history that is being taught to us these temple complexes were destroyed methodically by Arabs somewhere between 7th to the 14th century, then how did this statue reach Germany intact and absolutely preserved when Germany never ruled India.

Literally every Western Capital has in their historical records noted the input from all British East India Company logs: From the years 1847-1947, every single day a whopping 200 tons of gold removed from India by British. This number works out to a fantastic 6 million tons of Gold, taken out of India by the EIC in the 100 year interval. A fraction of this was used for financing every war, the destruction of China, as well as the destruction of every aspect of India.

Just as with the recent de-monetization, the ploy of the Western Economic apparatus pushed upon the Indians is "show publicly 0.25 Trillion USD, and hide 3.75 Trillion USD from public view", the case with Gold is show 160,000 tons and hide the larger figure of 6-million tons. But nevertheless, note again that according to the records, they are supposed to have looted be much less than 30% of the existing wealth from the temples looting, and confiscating from the Kingdoms and their treasuries. Further, this is only the Gold, this is apart from other Jewelry (precious stones, diamonds etc). This 6 million tons of gold is worth about 180 Trillion USD. By way of comparison, the Institute of International Finance figures the World debt at 217 Trillion USD, more than three times the World's GDP. (The IIM-professors, who realized the importance of the bullock-carts, may please enlighten us: how did we mine these 6 million tons before the British came? Did we seek any foreign help?)

So still 70% is left with India, so by this estimate, we have about 14 million Tons of Gold still left in India...counting only gold......not counting precious jems etc...... No wonder India is called the "Ratna Garbha". This gold is still with the people and with the temples. Then instead of 1 pound today being set at 70 Rupees, if India were to back its rupee with the gold that we have, the inverse case would be the reality viz: 1 Rupee = 70 British Pounds. Simply put, the amount of gold still left in India is valued at around two times the World's total Debt. Who wouldn't want to ROB IT??

In 2010 the minister for the mines Dasari Narayana Rao gave a written reply to the Parliament that there are 8.8 million oz of minable gold in one single block D-51/D-52?? of Anantapur District. At roughly 30 oz = 1 kg, this is 0.3 million Kilograms = 300 tons. What of the hundreds of other such blocks? The minister held his head high and stated with pride that since India does not have the technology to mine this gold, so we give the contract it to foreign countries.

All the economic indicators and the leading economists and financial experts are saying that the Anglo-American world has blown-up its gold reserves. That is why neither Bank of England nor Federal Reserve want any audit, because it will prove that there is no gold there. Many economists actually suspect that the gold mining figures themselves might have been cooked up and as the value of the gold-prices shooting up, both Fed and Bank of England, sold all their gold reserves to the gold-hungry world, primarily India and China. It is precisely this process that kept their currencies at stable value.

Though initially there were no physical gold transfers executed, recently many countries have started asking for the physical gold into their territories. The Chinese and Germans had requested the Federal Reserve to repatriate the physical gold to their countries. Both were duped and the gold was replaced with other metals.

Many of these countries which believe in the geopolitical objective of a multi-polar world, declared that they would de-link their currency with the dollar and link it with the gold –starting with Iran, Iraq, Libya, Syria, China and now Russia. In the last two decades of wars in the world, the question of currency-linkage has been the critical causative trigger. All the wars occurred exactly when the countries said that they are going to pull out of the dollar and back their currency with Gold. Whether it was the invasion of Iraq or Libya or Syria, or the current sabre-rattling going on with Russia and with China, all these were and are exactly because these countries had the courage to state that they were pulling out of the dollar and moving to a gold-standard. In addition to direct confrontation, the Anglo-American world resorted to a variety of financial frauds to the rigging of stocks, to the interest-rate-manipulation called Libor Scandal, in which the Europeans held the Bank of England guilty and were about to press large fines whereupon Britain exited from the European Union.

The main cause of the financial ruin in the interval 2008-2012 was this currency manipulation, without any gold left top back it up. If the countries are not of European origin, they are all subjected to what we can now call as gold-pipeLine wars in which Iraq and Libya are knocked out and promptly their gold-reserves were confiscated. And the world is witnessing the similar brink-of-war situation with the other four powers, which were accused by the Anglo-Americans of cornering most of the Gold in the last decade: namely China, Syria, Iran, Russia and North Korea.

As realized in the Syrian adventure is that the outcome of the war is uncertain. However, the serious financial crisis the US and the UK are facing is certain. They need gold urgently to save their financial system and economies and the very integrity of their financial institutions like Bank of England and the Federal Reserve. Thus, they need the gold for two reasons: to fight the wars and to maintain their own institutions.

We are looking at a staggering figure of 20-30 Trillion dollars worth of Gold, or the equivalent amount of real currency to buy such Gold. So then, the obvious question is:- "Apart from the other six nations we have to fight, Who has the currency or who has the Gold?" The answer is obvious: Only India. So therefore as a first shot, 4-Trillion dollars were taken out and as the next logical step, they will come behind the gold of the Individuals that is stored in India, as the East India Companies have done over the past 100 years.

If in the future, some Indian ruler had the courage to declare that the Indian currency would henceforth be backed by Gold, Indians may please rest assured that **India would have to be declared a terrorist country**. They would then have to fight with India. Here is the problem:- Fighting with 1.25 billion people is not the same as fighting with Iraq, Libya or with Syria. So, thus therefore a **three-pronged strategy** has been adopted: First, degrade the Indian Army to a fourth-class, un-professional and highly-politicized Army. This is precisely following the theory of the General Wellesley Clarke Under which goes under the title of the Strategic Defense Initiative. This will ensure that at any future point of time, if we have to fight with India, it will be an impotent India. Second, move to take the Gold physically out of India so that, we the Indians, can never at any future point of time, use it to back up our currency. One way to take the Gold out is to generate much more black money inside India and take that money out of India....this money being convertible to the Indian Gold. This is where our Government knowingly or unknowingly is falling prey to Western Economic theories of Thuggery and Robbery by demonetizing and re-introducing the much higher currency with a much higher denomination, and only just one reason why the Public are not being shown any consistent steps to handle the question of Indian currency being printed abroad.

Thirdly, push the Indian elite away from understanding and from original thought. And if we see how the Indian research institutes are being forced to lower standards, scientists getting badly de-motivated in research, reduced in quality, funding, strength, finally towards closure and shutting down, we can see India racing on the lines of Destruction. In fact, they never really needed to fight with India, because India was never a republic. It was never that "India is Independent"—rather it has always been "India is in-dependence". To control the slaves who had thus been deprived of independent enquiry and thought, the foreign masters need only slogans. India is not a democracy, it is a sloganocracy, the slogans trumpeted by the press-titutes of the private media corporate media.

Several American Presidents have publicly declared that the Corporate Media is a Fake Media. The White House has itself declared that all Corporate Media establishments, such as CNN, ABC, LA-Times, NY-Times which are the Fake Media have no access to the White House. But, we Indians lap up news from this same Corporate Media as if it were the Gospel Truth.

Only one simple example of this fake media's method of confusing the public of both India and Partitioned India – aka Pakistan –, was on the surgical strikes the army was supposed to have conducted with regard to the Kashmir question. CNN-India ran a program in their Prime-Time and showing that they were taking a call from a Pakistani General from the Neelam Valley who confirmed the strikes, the Indian Public were shown that India had in-fact executed the Surgical Strikes, and then CNN-India went on to push the slogan that whoever opposed the Surgical Strikes are not patriotic Indians and were anti-nationals.

But exactly at the same time, CNN-Pakistan aired a Program which was shown to the Pakistanis in which they had taken Journalists to the same Neelam valley and convinced the People of Pakistan that India has NOT conducted any surgical Strikes at all. And the experienced Pakistani Generals mused and bewildered that if the arc of operational radius of the Surgical Strikes as projected by India of radius 260 Km, this would be logistically tantamount to a not to a "Surgical Strike" but to a "Major Aerial Warfare". But yet, following CNN-India lead, every other private funded corporate media carried on the same line for one week, insisting that anyone who opposes their message is anti-national.

We are not questioning the capability of the Indian Air-force in conducting such operations, nor are we questioning that a firm hand is necessary in tackling the menace of Terrorism. But what we are questioning is whether the Indian public should accept at all what the Corporate Media is telling them. And as to what really happened there, the nation has a right to know....

While the simple hard working folk of India, who push voting buttons based on what they hear, certainly have a "right to know", a valid question to the moral authorities of the so-called "higher-educated" India: **is it our RIGHT TO KNOW......OR is it OUR DUTY TO FIND OUT?** The part of Indian society that is supposed to work cerebrally has badly failed its duty. It is time for this section to realize this and get to work again......when everyone else in the country is working.

What a tragic twist of fate for a country which claims to have given the Artha-Shastra to the world —this same Artha-Shastra was and being is duly followed to the letter in every Western Country, including in Pakistan, and yet waiting to be utilized for the betterment of the Indian economics.

CHAPTER TWELVE

Of MuttaaDhiPatis, PeethaDhiPatis & Allied Gangsters

We shall choose two examples to illustrate the decadence of the spiritual establishment in India. The first is the more recent, and the second is the more serious backdrop.

The complete corrupting of the religious and spiritual establishment of India from its relatively humble, morally-upright and ethically un-compromising stand, started with the first de-monetization attempt in India. This corruption scandal which might as well be called "**Saffron-Gate**", is probably larger than any other corruption scandal in the World, enabling India to occupy the Number-1 position in spiritually-corrupted countries all over the world—a distinction we have not achieved in any other field.

When the first demonetization occurred, every high-denomination note above Rs 100 was declared void, but unlike in the current de-monetization the voided higher currencies were not re-introduced and thus the very purpose of the first de-monetization was not defeated. With this nullification the black money hoarders panicked unlike in the current de-monetization.

But many of the religious institutions approached the authorities and requested an exemption for themselves so that they could deposit all the cash they had which was offered to them by way of donations by spiritually and religiously- minded God-fearing devotees of various states. As these "poor spiritual-religious-institutions" generally did not care about how much money they received, the Government exempted them from the regular limits on currency deposits which were imposed on individuals or corporations at that time in India.

However, this exemption born from a genuine understanding of the mode-of-operation of the religious and spiritual institutes was turned into a mega-fraud by the nexus of Political-Corporate-Industrial -criminals. A percentage-deal was cut with the religious institutes by the black money holders, in which the black money was donated to these spiritual institutions who in turn converted the entire black-money into white using the special privilege and then retained a percentage of it for themselves and returned the balance converted white money to the same black-money holders. The fraction retained by the religious institutions amounted to thousands of crores of Rupees.

Following this, these religious institutes became full-fledged mafias investing their suddenly gotten fortunes into real-estate and allied commercial activities. Some entrepreneurial ones went multi-national and becoming in general Black Money launders of other religious institutes and of politicians , creating massive amounts of wealth and commercial ventures outside India, especially in US, Canada, New Zealand, England and numerous small islands-to name a few. A comprehensive list of such people was offered to the Government of India, including the names of many businessmen associated with them, by the German Government which was investigating the Bank Frauds and taxation, and also by the few investigators while searching for the truth in the Panama Papers as recently as 2015.

Every notable leader of all political/religious/spiritual establishment who beat their chest at the first available instance, while proclaiming to bring the black money back into India and to stop corruption, has literally refused to touch this list which was offered to us by the German Government and by the investigative journalists.

The Enforcement directorate over the last five or six years determined that many and most of the Indian religious institutions are the recipients of thousands of Crores of Rupees from outside which were neither audited, nor subject to public scrutiny including by the institutional members. No cases filed, no punishments handed out.

It is alleged that the Indian Army has its hand invisibly tied in dealing with the Kashmir problem. Going back to the start of the creation of the Kashmir Problem, when the Indian army was just about to take over the Sharada Valley, with the SharadaSarvajna Peetha—the ancient Universal Center for Learning in Kashmir being a mere four km away, the Indian army contended that they were prevented from doing so by the British. Strangely enough though, it was at the time un-guarded.

This SharadaSarvajnaPeetha was one of the major cultural-educational-spiritual centers not only for Kashmir but also of the world at large. It attracted scholars of repute for millennia the world over. For centuries together, it was stated in India that one's education can only be complete after visiting the ShardaSarvjanaPeeta and get accredited by them. From Sankaracharya to Ramanujacharya, one and all visited this sacred cultural Zion of India in Kashmir before expounding their philosophies to the public.

It may be anecdotally mentioned that the Pakistani army is currently preserving it as a cultural heritage center and scholars from Pakistan have been requesting the Government of India to permit Indian scholars and archeologists and spiritual scholars to join hands with them and to resurrect this University Center of Learning to its ancient Glory. **But having got fed up with the colossal apathy of both the spiritual, political and religious establishments of India,** in an attempt to ward off the destruction of the remainder of the SharadaSarvajnaPeeta by the international jihadi groups, **the Pakistanis finally appealed to the UN to take it over as a heritage site.** This paved the way for German and Russian archeologists to study the extent of this university of the world's ancient center of learning.

By the way, the current King of Kashmir, who stays at Delhi, advises against worrying about this vast complex at all — reasoning "there are many other temples in Kashmir which we can look towards". It would certainly be a valid question if one asked about the motive for the Indian Army's "Surgical Strikes" focused around this Sarada Valley/Neelum Valley area. **Let the Indians note that none of the PeethaDhiPatis either of the Vaishnavite or the Shaivite Order or MuttaDhipathis or the Sri Vidya Upasakas, or any other Indian Religious Leaders either consciously or unconsciously, either in wakeful state or their dream state, even raise the faintest of protests asking our Government to restore this greatest ancient center of learning** where for the first time massive bodies of knowledge were committed to writing in the Sarada Script, which became an authentic source for most of the religious leaders to propound their philosophical doctrine.

The British by back-door maneuvering deliberately prevented the Indian Army from taking over this seat of learning, due to what they recognized was the in-estimable value of this SarvajnaPeetha. Let it also be noted that the Indian army did-not and/or was-not-allowed-to secure and control a critical center storehouse of vast amounts of knowledge.

This single failure alone indicates that even prior to the Saffron-Gate, **a deep loss of awareness about our knowledge bases had already set into the Indian spiritual orders, most of them having by now lost the ability to claim themselves as Peetadhipatis or Muttadhipatis,** in the proper sense of the term.

It is also to be noted, albeit on a different note, that this is **but one of many examples** where the **Indian army** has at all times been**following the orders of Back-Door-British-Maneuvered Indian-Politicians to defend British-defined borders, rather than** take it upon themselves to **defend and protect critical centers of social, scientific and spiritual learning.**

The absolutely desperate situation of the various religious spiritual orders in India is also reflected in their abject failure to identify exactly the geographical locations as clearly referred to in our recent or ancient geographical texts, and circle instead around theories pushed by the British that all of these were somehow, defying all common-sense, restricted to the borders of present-day India...subtly implying that the current British-drawn borders are actually divinely ordained, the Indian public being drugged with this self-delusionary exclusive-divinity, their spiritual leadership unable to shake off the effects of this most dangerous delusion.

We have not yet heard one full authoritative and consistent explanation, that will satisfy our scientists, from our scriptural establishments that will objectively resolve for example the question of the Rama setu and the Hanuman Jump, Yojana-to-mile conversion issue, resulting a discrepancy of a geographical factor of about 60. We may have at best heard some sketchy ones that are badly incomplete.

For another example, out of the hundred and eight ShaktiPeethas mentioned and indentified in our texts, only 54 are to be found within the current British-Created Geographical borders of India. The rest of them are outside currently-defined India and even as of today no one knows where they are. Let it be stated that, as seen above, the known primary SharadaSarvajnaPeeta Kshetra was not taken back into India. We do not hear any Scriptural Authorities in India giving a reasoned opinion, or for that matter, any opinion at all on this issue.

And again of all, post-partition and "independence", many of those critical cultural heritage centers that could tell us who we actually are, and help is to correctly understand our history, existed in Pakistan (West India). These were dismantled (either physically or by spreading false stories) and then re-located back inside the British-Divided India, in most cases by creating artificial stories and rumors around temples & centers existing in current-day India. The wiser thing to have done would have been for us to have a dialog with our Western Cousins, the Pakistanis, and leave the sacred places on their original geographic locations as they are doing for the Nanak's birthplace and for a few others.

The place where Lord Narasimha appeared is called Moolasthana or Multan is now located in Pakistan. Rather than opening a discussion our Western Cousins (aka Pakistanis), and maintain the temple's locational-sanctity there, and attempt to understand the true time-scales and geographical context of the Narasimha, we abandoned it and re-located the temple's story to another temple in the Cuddapah district of Andhra Pradesh. In the same breath the Odyana Peetha, which was one of the primary centers of Shakti worship was in Swat Valley Pakistan, was abandoned and re-located to Odisha after Partition. None in India ever made any attempts to communicate with our cousins, the Pakistanis (West Indians) to preserve the locational geographical sanctity of these structures.

In fact, the Pakistani government has declared them as UN heritage sites, including the Aditya temple in Multan. That there is no discussion whatsoever on these critical issues, shows that the so-called Indian spiritual leadership has lost all of its abilities to either follow the path of spiritualism or to guide the people of India on the path of spirituality. Instead, they have chosen to become commercial, multi-branded retail outlets for spiritualism, more interested than politicians in preserving and perpetuating their commercial and political interest, at times fighting pitched battles on the streets with guns and weapons for the succession struggles of the Peethas.

If the Indian armed Forces do not recognize and represent themselves to protect the cultural/spiritual/academic/knowledge-based heritage of India, but concern themselves only with British-Created-Borders, **it only indicates how badly dis-oriented the Armed Forces are at their highest level in terms of understanding their true role** in the defense of the country.

CHAPTER THIRTEEN

Time Travel: India 2040 – Prime Minister Sigmund Freud?

Our Respected Honorable Prime Minister Shri Narendra Modi, has recently made a public statement advising the younger generation to talk openly about depression. To supportive Indians who are rightly concerned about the well-being of country and of our Prime Minister, may we please be aware that more than one American President has been known to experience severe mental health problems while in office, many times verging on nervous-breakdowns...In this regard, we may bring to notice the choice made by President Bill Clinton, who was advised to seek Psychiatric help post the Monica Lewinsky scandal, declined and chose instead to seek the support of Christian Ministers.

No secret here, but what might come as a surprise to those, whether Indians or Americans, who treat Presidents as heroes, is that the pressures on the office of the President from the various Geopolitical Forces must be tremendous ones to endure. Citizens of a country would do well to assist their leader in this process, by understanding the forces that the leader is subject to, rather than to deify and worship the leader and expect him to work miracles as is commonly done in several countries, including in India.

We are in a sense very much on the same page as our Prime Minister, as you may have gauged from the title of this booklet. We recognize the critical role of the mind, although in our publication, we are more concerned about the social mind. Certainly, we would like to talk about the problem. The only question is ...talk to whom?

Certainly not to a bunch of ignoramuses called psychologists, who are commonly known to be good-for-nothing, who go to colleges giving corrupting lectures to the younger generation on Boy-Girl relations, who even today are basing themselves on teachings of Sigmund Freud — whose fraudulent theories are so vulgar, and their implications so devastating to society that we don't want to repeat Sigmund Freud's theories in a section associated with our Respected Prime Minister — but please may we inform that a large section of **God-fearing American Society has already been destroyed by the theories of Sigmund Freud? And that the vast majority of Indians who view America ape precisely this destroyed component?** Precisely because their English-based education system could not teach them any better? No certainly it would be unwise to talk to them.

Depression is merely a call from our deeper self asking ourselves to wake-up to it, telling us that too many unwanted processes are running in our mind, and that it is time to clean up and to come back to the reality. Thus, therefore it is a very good teacher. The question is how do we react to it? Do we listen to its deeper warnings and search its deeper significance or do we try to push it away by increasing the dose of medicines created by Corporate America, somewhat like kicking your own teacher?

It is very true that there may be individuals in all walks of life who face depression, but History is not much about individual suffering. Although the suffering may be bad, the suffering of a depression 'victim' is not to be compared with the suffering of millions of dead soldiers and their families, of farmers pushed to work as urban labor because their agricultural land has been robbed or their agriculture otherwise destroyed, of starving children etc.

Individual suffering has no meaning here. The higher goal is to understand the individual suffering in order to give meaning to society. Thus, therefore, we shall choose to sacrifice the question of individual depression to the cognitive-dissonance that our society is now in. It is precisely our case that the cognitive-dissonance that has taken over India, if allowed to worsen will result in what can be called "severe social depression" on a massive scale, this term to be understood as being far more severe than "economic depression". Thus, it is our case that we should do our best to correct our cognitive-dissonance before this hits us.

The collective (and also individual) mind is impacted by the Public Education system and by the social expectations both of which aspects have in and of themselves been confused in our society. As far as the education system is concerned, cognitive-dissonance is the early-warning sign to re-sacralize our education system and pull out of systems that are now moving towards dangerous de-sacralization. Once again, as far as social expectations are concerned, cognitive-dissonance is the early-warning call to pull back from the artificially created hype and to understand who we actually are in relation to our society. (If the ancient wisdom of all lands is correct, the correct understanding who we are is precisely the re-sacralization of the education system itself.)

Very simply put, collective state of minds is related to state of society. The state of society is related to social institutions. Social institutions depend on direction from head of the institution. The heads of all Indian institutions have either become directionless, or are accepting that they are losing direction. In this directionless system the younger generation is has no other choice and is forced to accept the dangerous ideologies being pushed by the Western Corporates.

We particularly warn our readers that while technology has several positive and utilitarian aspects, pushing **"Digital India"** in the current configuration of Indian society which has a very poor understanding of geo-political issues, **will result in a sharp increase of this cognitive-dissonance**, and cause you to take the wrong decisions or prevent you from taking any decision. What is worse, it will cause you to outsource your decision making process. In **contrast strengthening "Mathematical India" and "Historical India" and "Social India" and "Cultural India" will positively act to reduce the cognitive dissonance** which will help you to make conscious choices, in the current time and space — hopefully if we understand what current time and space we are in — that will decide the existence and continuation of India as a republic, and as a state and will help regain its Glory as a center of Universal Cultural Heritage and learning, making it a true Global Village that will solve, resolve every problem that exists in the world today, be it at any level.

The most critical danger facing us at the highest levels of our social mind is the Loss of our locational awareness in space-time. One visible symptom of the loss in awareness of location in time is manifested in the fact that we are not able to come up with a hundred-year blueprint for our country, while the plans of all other major geopolitical players are several times that long. One visible symptom of the loss of awareness in spatial-location is that we do not know our geographic context in relation to our society (which is why our confused Party spokespersons say look East, no Look West, no,no, Look North etc) and our complete in-ability to read geopolitical threats coming from the various directions.

Perhaps, one serious mistake we may have committed is to assume that space-time is a concept that only Physicists ought to study. **No, here we are wrong.** There is a social view on both space as well as on time. While, this would theoretically require the study of space-time to be conducted by the History Departments, the pitiable History departments of India's educational institutions are tragically, woefully, hopelessly in-adequate for this task.

It is our endeavor in this brief section to outline the historical forces that have caused our society to lose the awareness of space-time and of our location in it. Primarily we shall point a key element which is a conflict between the British, the Church, the FreeMasonic Orders and the French — in the context of which India became a victim.

A critical basis in the understanding of psychology is the axiom that the human being is a social being. The society you live in and the people around you, you family, your elders, the social figures influence your thought processes to a very great degree. In India, it is very fortunately still the case, that a vast majority of people do not exhibit behavior that opposes the norms of society. However, a degree of confusion is being created by images of a highly individualized West, and this effort has been in some good measure successful.

Indians would do well to understand that the highly individualized approach to society as being pushed and practiced in Western Societies is not their natural state. It is actually the result of a tinkering of their education systems for the last hundred years, dating back to the classical problem of the fight between the Church and its enemies, primarily various aspects of the Free-Masonic orders. In this battle-to-the-death, first the latter then the former, realized correctly that the while the foe cannot be changed, the "one who will become the foe" can be changed.

This led to an attempt in Europe to control the minds of younger generations by attempting two things: 1) Push in perceptions and limit information receiving abilities, twist the published information to suit the pushed perception. 2) Manipulate the process whereby the received information is re-enforceable as being true and valid. Particularly, the second point explains why a large number of Indian students feel that the Social Studies in India are useless, the information they are receiving is completely disconnected from the observed reality, making it impossible for the mind to validate.

So, the British-created establishment controlled what we might call the 4 P's: the Public school system, the Printing, the Public Debate as mediated by the Government, and the Press.

Indians should note that the strategy applied by the Free-Masons in attacking the Church was used against India by a combination of the Church and the British, who had by now learned and mastered the art. Let it be noted that the starting point of this dilemma was the French Revolution. **The French rejected the attempt by the Church to push the fraudulent time- and spatial- lines on them, precisely because they had a direct source of the true time- and space- lines from India.** This is in fact the root of the French revolution, culminating with the Rise of Napoleon who crowned himself Emperor as opposed to getting crowned by the Pope.

But, if these ideologies were allowed to run, the Church would have been destroyed by now. The fact that this has not happened, indicates that they have fought back.

The battle ground of this fight was India and America. One of the side-effects of holding the Church in check in America was an extreme individualization of Philosophies etc which is perhaps the only side (–the worse side at that) the Indian public are shown about America today by the Corporate media. In India however the fight took a different turn. Unlike America of the time, India had a vast knowledge-base that was very much alive. So, in India then, the British colluded with the Church to completely destroy the Indian knowledge base.

A major factor for the British, for taking the path of discrediting everything in India as worthless, thus, subjugating populations to mental spiritual servitude, came from the intellectual thinking of revolutionary France. Having had trade connections with India for very long before the advent of British, the French had translated, from the Sanskrit and other Indian languages, many treatises on mathematics, science and medicine in to French. This made them understand the importance of mathematics and science in relation to society. In particular, the French realized the most unscientific basis of the public version of Christianity with its tale of the creation tale of genesis, dating the entire evolution of universe to few thousands of years.

By scientifically rejecting the absurdity of religion, the French moved to reject Christianity as main social binding force during the revolution, specifically citing Indian astronomical accounts. From Voltaire to several others, this trend became a bed rock in forging the French revolution based on intellectual achievements and self-knowledge with slogans of equality, liberty and fraternity. This shift from the Church to a Republic shook the very foundations of Catholicism.

This popped up an unusual alliance between British and Catholic Church to disprove the French and the nascent German thinking about the role of knowledge in statecraft. More specifically, the Church and the British concerned themselves with the problem of how to discard and disprove such knowledge if it went against the established dogmas of church. The British struck an alliance with the Catholic Church to complete the task of discarding of Oriental knowledge in favor of that of the Church and their time-lines in exchange for agreement of non-competition with them in trade with the Indian subcontinent.

Since the beginning of 1785 a systematic methodology was adapted by British to achieve their objective of intellectual spiritual and mental enslavement of Indians. This was long before Macaulay presented his plan in British Parliament. And by 1815, with the defeat of Napoleon in the battle of Waterloo, the British eliminated all French presence from India.

Let Indians also note that Continental Europe has always treated the British as Pirates, and the British were kept out of all civilized activities. Now the British, who were always treated as Pirates, wanted to show to continental Europe that they were also civilize, pro-Science, pro-advancement. To this end, they adopted the charade of civilizing others and the British and the Church entered into an un-holy agreement. Note that the Church was the victim of the French Revolution based on the French Renaissance, that was actually based on the Astronomical knowledge the French obtained from India.

So the agreement of this unholy alliance was that if the British could find a find a way to check-mate France and counter the French danger to the Church, in return the Church would see to it that the British would be admitted to the Empire and would not be treated as pirates.

And it is precisely the effect of this unholy alliance that we will see at all points in India....Note once again that Indian Astronomical Knowledge was the main danger to the Church via the French Revolution..... The vast percentage of Europeans who came to learn the Veda as scholars were Catholics, whereas their British controllers and financiers were Protestants. Thus, therefore, the British adopted a two-pronged strategy. First, militarily check-mate the French by throwing up coalition after coalition, AND secondly, destroy the source of the knowledge that has created the French

Revolution....this led to the destruction of knowledge bases in India.

Destruction of the knowledge-bases in India was a four-pronged approach. First, destroy the funding sources to all centers of learning in India. Second corner all manuscripts and lift them out of India. Third, raze to the dust anything that survives in India in the form of astronomical observatories, temples, scientific marvels, plunder and pillage them (and put the complete blame on the Muslims) so that future Indian generations will never be able to re-construct the truth about what has happened to them. A careful campaign was launched to discredit all traditional modes of learning in India and both Sanskrit and Persian were pushed down. The British had realized that most of the Indian traditional texts had been already translated into the Persian and the Persian translations too would have to be destroyed. Fourthly, prevent the Indian mind from going back to the process of re-construction of their destroyed History by completely re-engineering their ideas of space and time.

They retrofitted the entire time-line of the "Indian" civilization to 2-3000 B.C. They tinkered historical texts available in India to limit their geographical location to within British India. When they carefully controlled the archives, the libraries, public education system, they published only 636-odd texts, out of the hundreds of thousands of manuscripts that were taken out. These 636-odd texts are then used to show that there was no Indian civilization worth the name. The 636 texts were used to push a Christian thought on the Indian mind, and created a new religion. The followers of this new religion were called **HINDUS= Her-majesty's INdians, DUmb and Stupid**.

The whole of Continental Europe, especially the French and the Germans decried this massive onslaught on the Indian knowledge base that was being perpetuated by the British. But with the political turmoil in Europe no other country was able to interfere to checkmate the British onslaught. With nobody, including the Indians, to oppose them, the British attempted to set the entire Indian civilizational anchor points into a biblical frame work of 2000 years BC. This convoluted the Indian mind to the time-frame of biblical creation tales at 5000 years.

From the oldest texts available, the Vedas to everything else was retrofitted in to this 5000 year time frame work and piped to the masses through the public education system in a manner made to appear matter of fact. The Indian mind with an intellect unable to question this onslaught and in the absence of sources of knowledge or having no means to retrieve these sources, slowly surrendered their basic quality of questioning to seek truth and began to simply accepting passively whatever was being taught to them.

The new religion, Hinduism, which is absolutely hierarchical, oppressive and which fostered an ignorance, that brooked no questioning, was piped in to the brains of one and all starting with school children, with women being relegated to positions of slaves.

A critical role in the destruction of the society in India was played out with the destruction of the state of women. The British pushed the case that women are not equal to men and have no property rights and changed the succession rules so that property can be inherited by male offspring only. Thus, the role of women in the society was confined to baby-producing machines or physical objects dependent on the man, and cut them off from all critical social spheres. This was the copy of the Christian thought.

With no way to learn what the ancient texts actually said, as the traditional learning centers were destroyed, the Indian Mind violently swung between contradictory pictures of woman are being divine to being sex slaves. It finally ended up paying lip service to women being embodiment of some god-head but accepted the new found position of male superiority. From being represented by a Brahmin widow Queen Rani Lakshmibai, leading a great war against the best of the best British generals (Cornwallis), the last fifty years have seen women relegated to objects of servitude attending to household duties.

So, for example on the specific question of women, the Indian mind is thus forced to oscillate between three contradictory anchors. One is what they are taught in fragments from history coming down traditionally. The second is what they are taught by the Public Education System. The third is the observed reality in the world today. The three are completely irreconcilable. They have seen their grandmothers having property rights, participate in decision making processes, they have their grandmothers supporting a Brahmin Widow (Rani Laxmi Bai) and ruling a kingdom and fighting the best of the best of the British generals for several months. Contrasted to this is a legal reality, where women have no inheritance rights at all, again in contrast, they are taught that Western lead reforms have given equal rights to modern day Women. This dichotomy or Trichotomy between Rani Laxmi Bai and the current Judicial Position on women, and between what is taught to us in the public education system, is confusing our attitudes towards women in our society. ONE which we cannot prove, cannot look up to because we seem unable to move towards it, the SECOND of painful humiliation and the THIRD which goes against the nature of our mind to accept and is convoluted beyond reason.

If we accept the input from our historical memory (eg Rani Laxmi Bai), we are unable to prove it, and what is harder seem pitifully unable to get back to this state, of having a woman ruler who could challenge the British might (except briefly Mrs Indira Gandhi). If we accept the current judicial position, we can't live with it because it perpetuates the suffering of women. If we accept what is taught to us in the public school system, we immediately reject it because of the confusion it creates between history and the current reality.

As long as this is taught in the public schools, the confusion in the mind goes on increasing, because it contradicts the reality. In this confused state, we make a decision based on immediate survival in the present...in the manner of a slave who has to eat in order to survive.

When the British created the new religion of Hinduism, the reform movements and spiritual movements which although were calculated to show a carefully calibrated streak of nationalistic pride, the heads of these movements were geared to imitate their masters, the British. So the product of these social institutions, be they Hindu or Muslim or Reform are subject to this same confusion. All spiritual, political, religious, cultural leaders have come through this same system where the 4-Ps have been controlled and are they themselves directionless.

The followers of this new religion, called Hinduism, were pushed to such fraudulent institutions and fake teachers, and were convinced to follow an utterly impractical and even abusive spiritualism, that is inwardly useless and requires practices that are outwardly expensive and show no external results re-producible in a scientific manner. Our own Enforcement directorate has pointed out that most of these spiritual and religious institutions have today become major conduits of black money, creating a (un)holy alliance of politicians, industrialists and black money holders and of foreign Intelligence agencies.

A youngster, confused by a society that demands worships of white hair but which insults Time which caused the hair to grow white, goes to a confused spiritual leader who is a by-product of either the malevolent British-created fraudulent spiritual system or of the destroyed traditional system, can only expect to be further confused. Is it then our Honorable Prime Minister's case that the individual should go to a psychologist who has also been confused by the same system, who knows nothing about the context of societies in which the psychological theories they are taught arose?

The effect of this mental subjugation has resulted in clueless bureaucracy, a directionless army, senseless legal procedures of British era, and purposeless Intelligence Services. Though many in these fields honestly trying to do something good their number is very low and is fast disappearing. The only ones in India who are not confused are the British-created political class who became a mirror image of the British EIC officers whose single-minded purpose is like that of their British masters: to make enough money for at least 600 generations down the line at the expense of the common citizens.

True it is that for a brief period after independence, we attempted to repair this situation in many fields. But this phase was short-lived in the time-scales of History, and with the onset of Privatization and Liberalization, this same 4Ps are now back again with a vengeance and are pushing us back on the path of complete servitude and slavery.

Except that the British-engineered 4Ps post-liberalization are now being Privatized. is now post-Liberalization being done by another set of 4-Ps. The Public education system replaced by Private Education system, the Press replaced by Private Press, the Public Archives replaced by Private University Libraries and the Public Debate replaced by Private Corporate channel controlled debate. In this manner then, our psychology stemming from the dimensions of our social and historical control points was pushed downhill. Since liberalization the line of attack has been from British-controlled corporations in the name of "Privatization of Education System". And in continuation of the line pushed on us in the past, that we Indians have nothing worth the name, today our politicians gleefully admit in Parliament that we don't have any technical capabilities or knowledge, so we have to bring in foreign companies to mine our own gold and diamonds. And so it is history repeating again with the British controlled corporate bodies re-occupying India yet again, this time not as East India Company but via the Multinational Operated Destruction of India.

We have been taught that we have nothing to offer, our history is less than 5000 years old, that we have no cultural values, any culture is given to you by foreigners. We were slowly but methodically conditioned to accept that whatever is English IS Science and that what is NOT English is NOT Science; and on our socio-political front, we were conditioned to accept that the West is equivalent to English.

We hope it is not our Honorable Prime Minister's case that the younger generation talk to good-for-nothing "social scientists" or "psychologists" who are conditioned in the above manner, and cannot do much more than corrupt the younger generation by talking about "boy-girl" relationships. No, that would be terribly wrong and devastating for our society. Instead, we request our Respected Prime Minister to address the root of the problem.

Respected Prime Minister, do you have in your vast and varied country **just one** good psychologist in the country who can please talk about a Teacher-Student relationship —the core of your society—not boy-girl relationships please for God's sake !!

Respected Prime Minister, please find for the younger generation **just one** such psychologist in your country who can please stand up and tell the scientific and educational establishment in the country as to **what is the effect of language on the mind** and **what will happen to the minds of students when the Teacher-Student relationship in your country is functioning in English — a language that is neither the student's, nor the teacher's, nor the state's, nor determined by either Scientific procedure, nor by democratic procedure, but pushed on us by fraud?**

True, in our current school curricula there are some attempts being made in our books to make half-hearted attempts to teach Sanskrit or other languages and to make a passing mention of Aryabhatta or Ramanujan, but these are mere fleeting illusions and far from anything substantial or solid. We point to the strange dichotomy where English-medium educated graduate level physics students can understand the mathematics of the planetary orbits, but are unable to give even a single clue as to how the Panchang has been determined and continues to be determined with amazing accuracy, the Panchang tables being perhaps more easily available, and perhaps more widely used in India than commonly used log-tables; and vice versa too.

Thus therefore instead of all the shouting about "Indian-Sciences" and sloganeering about "Vedic vimanas", and the "Pride of our ancient Past", **what would be a far more solid and concrete step to take in this direction would be for Indian Physics departments to follow up the course on advanced Classical Hamiltonian Mechanics, where students learn the basics of astronomical planetary orbital calculations with a course on calculation of the Calendar.** This should not be too difficult to do at all given that it is already being done!!

To destroy the Indian pride in their astronomical and mathematical knowledge British missionaries and administration paid huge bribes to a few scholars in Ujjain asking them to proclaim a date for an eclipse that was incorrect by two days. This was published in all the governor's almanacs and on that date millions gathered to glimpse the eclipse and to take holy dip in the rivers.

But when the eclipse did not occur in main river confluences, the carefully placed British agents and Catholic fathers trumpeted that Indian astronomical knowledge was fake and absurd to the schooled millions. And the British then informed the distraught faithful that according to superior British scientific calculations the eclipse would occur in next three days which proved true, to the amazement of the public.

This fraudulent act of psychological war on the Indian mind came to light only around 1985 through the writings of the German and French scholars who were conducting a study on retrospective reconciliation of astronomical facts. Even NASA's declaration a decade ago about adapting astronomical tables of India into their computations could not restore the lost sense of pride in the Indians even to this day.

The Europeans who decried the British destruction of Indian knowledge were appalled by the fraudulent methods adapted by British to destroy scientific knowledge. Witnessing this massive disruption of mind and psyche of the Indians, the Germans and French did what they could do best within their limitations. Knowing the greed of British, the French and Germans offered as much cash as possible to salvage anything of value from India. So for a full century the plundered wealth of India – from manuscripts to artifacts to statues were auctioned in London's famous auction centers – and dutifully the Germans and French paid for and bought them. But what shocked the Germans the most was that when they returned one such statue to the current Indian Prime Minister, not one single member in the Prime Minister's entourage asked the basic question: "how did the Germans get this statue in first place?"

The education system is meant to deliberately create and perpetuate this ignorance, confusion in which the mind does not know even what question to ask. This confusion is a prerequisite to get a job in our re-engineered society. Not only is our understanding of time-space analysis messed up, but also our understanding of modernity- versus-traditional is also messed up. This confusion prevents us from correctly understanding what should be the link between history, the present and the future; and between maintaining the protection of tradition and accepting the legitimate changes of modernity. This forces us to make choices on the basis of what is critical for our immediate survival in the manner of a slave.

India is now at a critical fork. We have two paths ahead of us. The **downward path** leads to de-sacralization of the education system, breakup of all social units, creation of fraudulent ones, administration the mental health by increasing the number of psychologists who are themselves confused by the same system who will indiscriminately prescribe imported pharmaceutical drugs, outsourcing of our social decision making process, our thought-processes getting either increasingly and painfully convoluted or increasingly numbed. Pulled away from our rooting knowledge most of which is already gone, but which will have been completely robbed, we will be unable to steer back. Fragmented knowledge will be given to us, by the Foreign Corporate bodies, limited to what is required to get us to work like slaves for them with every aspect of life being under their control. Like that of the Thracian slaves chained below deck: "We keep you alive to serve this ship. Row well and Live." So would be the fate of the Indians if we made this choice. Thus it is that we asked the question: "Time Travel: India 2040 Prime Minister Sigmund Freud?"

But **if we choose the upward path**, the harder more difficult, but correct one, we will have to re-understand and re-work our education system completely. We will properly understand our location in space-time. Instead of serving as slaves chained below the deck to row the pirate ships, we will be the guides who could help the rest of the world see a higher truth.

It is this choice that will decide the existence and continuation of India as a republic, and as a state and will help regain its Glory as a center of Universal Cultural Heritage and learning, making it a true Global Village that will solve and resolve every problem that exists in the world today, be it at any level.

CHAPTER FOURTEEN

The Indian Armed Forces: A Fate Worse Than Death

The burning and the destruction of Kashmir, which is rightly called the **"Abandoned Heart and Soul of Dead India"**, both spiritually as well as materially, started at least a century before we got *"independence"*. This process was initiated by the British and then perpetuated by the British-installed puppet Dogra Kings and subsequently perfected by both the Congress and by the British Janissary Party, also known in India as the BJP.

Starting from the looting of Maharaja's Ranjit Singh's treasure of which 99% is still un-accounted for (the remaining one percent, being preserved by the British) —–to the destruction of every Solar and Lunar Observatories built in the entire Kashmir Valley and to the widespread dilapidation and careful removal of all the millennia-old archaeological treasures of Kashmir and selling them to the highest bidder in London's museums and streets —– to the arming of mercenaries borrowed from Iran as Afghan tribesmen and occupation of one-third of Kashmir —- thus cutting off permanently India's access to its own silk route and trade route to the central Asia to the North, Europe to the West and towards North East to China, Mongolia and the Orient, thus preventing timeless flow of commerce from all directions of the world into India to learn the Universal values of the Indian culture.

This appalling destruction of humanity's heritage has been followed up over the last 50 years by perpetuating the occupation and destruction of the land and culture by every alphanumeric Jihadi group, well funded and trained by the same British who initiated the process and by extension, their American, and by the latter's proxy – the Mossad, all as part of the Great Game. However, instead of understanding this international dynamics correctly, the **cognitive dissonance** which has set into the Indian thought process causes us to have a psychotic view, resulting in **delusional Pakistan-Centered foreign- and defense- policies.**

In the last 25 years this interference has resulted in an absolute ethnic-cleansing on an un-precedented scale in the modern history of the World. Today, this space left by the ethnic-cleansing of Kashmir has been filled by jihadis of every shade and every country, draining the life and blood of India. Except in Kashmir City where between three to five thousand Indians of non-Jihadi origin, also known as Kashmiris remain. Literally every town in Kashmir is cleansed of Indians/Kashmiris. The only Indians that remain in Kashmir are those that are pro-Pakistani.

Literally every archaeological site, every temple, every treasure of timeless heritage value has to be guarded under the bayonets and the guns of the CRPF. Most of the total battalion strength of the CRPF is deployed into the Kashmir Valley to guard these – this is apart from the military strength. And literally for every 200 feet, machine gun wielding soldiers guard every turn.

Since last five years, the situation is worsening day-by-day. This worsening is not in the occupied part of Kashmir, but in the part that India controls. The occupation of the Indian side of Kashmir by the jihadi forces is almost total and maybe completed in the next five years. We have lost over 50,000 armed personnel in guarding these sites — double the number of casualties in all the five wars which India fought with its enemies — combined.

But even today, there is no end in sight. Forget about re-taking the occupied Kashmir, we may even lose the Indian occupied side in the next five years — thus confirming the fraudulently pushed view of the British Historians that Aryavarta ends before the Jhelum river.

Let us note here, that though no Americans were killed, as a preventive measure and to send a signal, we mention that the current Trump Administration has, in violation of every international law and pushing to the brink-of-war with Russia, launched 59 Tomahawk Missiles on Syria. By contrast, since 1946, close to 100,000 Kashmiris were killed, many women in the last 20 years were literally raped, their breasts chopped off, to kick one section of the population out of Kashmir, by cross-border terrorism, funded by the International Sponsors, which continues even today, over 50,000 military personnel have been killed and are being killed as of writing of this article. Trillions worth of property damage, invaluable, irreplaceable and possibly irreversible cultural and spiritual heritage has been wiped out, but yet not even a single coherent response to protect the lives and properties of Indians has ever either thought about or planned, leave alone put into action.

DO WE or DO WE NOT have a capability to SOLVE THE KASHMIR PROBLEM? Or do we want to burn the energy and resources, time and lives of the armed personnel and people just for the greed and corruption of few politicians of all different political parties and their political backers.

If we believe that our armed forces are in-capable of protecting us, **may we suggest a glance at how the Syrians responded to a similar problem**? Let us take a look.

60% of Syria has been occupied by the ISIS over the last 15 years, the ISIS being backed by a consortium of International Financiers, Colonial Masters, Drug-dealers, Arms and Antique traffickers. (By the way, the extent of the antique trafficking in Syria, which possessed less than 0.1% of the cultural antiques in Kashmir, is annually valued at 7-billion dollars and is carried out by the Jihadi groups. Every major western Capital is raising a hue and cry about the cultural destruction of Syria, which they call the cradle of the Middle-Eastern civilization. Then what about Kashmir — the cradle of the World Civilization — that has been burning for over 50 years?)

When Syrian government was unable to fight they did not let Syria burn to the state of the ethnic –cleansing of Kashmir. Nor did they allow thousands of their armed personnel to be killed like sheep while they are eating and sleeping, like what we allowed in Kashmir. Nor, after these thousands of deaths and years of insurgency, did the Syrians boast of a single surgical strike and then debate endlessly whether that strike was genuine or false.

When the Syrians realized the international dimension of the Jihadi problem, given the international colonial, neo-colonial, liberal geo-political dimension of the Jihadi problem, **they simply declared an all-out existential war of life and death**; and took the help of Iran and Russia to decisively solve the problem of insurgency, militancy and terrorism.

The Syrians are re-taking every inch of the land that has been illegally occupied since 15 years. They never went for a political settlement or deals for provincial-based electoral victories. For every Syrian soldier killed, a hundred Jihadis were taken down and finally they will pretty soon cleanse the entire Syria from the Colonial Created jihadi problem — re-conquering every inch of their land.

We challenge every group in India that claims to be patriotic to think in their wildest imaginations to at least begin to ponder such solutions to this 50-year-old never ending cycle of death-destruction-massacre-ethnic-cleansing-cultural-spiritual-eradication taking place in the Sovereign Democratic Republic of India. The most ridiculous part is that no government wants to talk about this problem. None in the rest of India are aware of what is happening there. Perhaps proper brokerage fees have not been agreed upon at an acceptable percentage for creating a "Make-In-India" Solution for Kashmir.

Has any defense analyst or Military Chief in India pondered over the possibility (however ridiculous it might appear): "It will be no wonder at all if within the next year **the Syrian army can offer to solve the jihadi problem in both the Indian-side and in the Pakistan Occupied side** — because of the vast experience they have had in cleansing the country from the various alphanumeric Jihadi groups and their international backers."?

Instead of attending to problems and cleaning up our public sector by- and in- itself, successive Governments in India have privatized a large portion of our public sector and given it to foreigners on the grounds that "the public-sector is in-efficient". **Who knows, for the right price, they may even decide to liberalize and privatize both the Indian Army as well as the solution to the Kashmir Problem?** We sincerely hope that the Indian army will stand up and fight against the allegation that it has failed to solve the Kashmir problem even though it had fifty years to do so....

While the Mathematicians at the Chennai Institute of Mathematical Sciences, and the Social Scientists at the Tata Institute of Social Sciences and Faculty Members of the IITs Academic departments will fully understand that you, the Armed Forces, are probably not entirely to blame. Unfortunately as illustrated above, they do not seem to be taken seriously either by our society or by our Government nor perhaps, having got fed up, do they take themselves seriously any longer.

Who knows that **contrasted to them the "Brand India", "India-for-sale", alcohol-intoxicated-dancing-drunken-disorderly public exemplified by the the midnight foreign-DJ Jazz concert in Bengaluru, will dance to the tune of the corporate media and sing songs written by the Indian Institute of Management (IIM) MBA-musicians asking for the Indian Army to be Liberalized and Privatized on the grounds that it has failed to do its job in Kashmir?**

While we pray to Dear God that this unfortunate state of events does not come to pass, in case it does we **please ask you that if you are privatized, please-pretty-please hand over the solving of the Kashmir Problem to the Syrian Tiger forces and NOT to anyone else**....certainly not to the Saudi Arabs or to the Omanis, who shared the dais with the BJP spokesperson in section 1...or in following the Hillary Clinton-advise of "India Look East" as suggested by the BJP spokesperson, certainly do not, in any event, outsource it to the Chinese.

We cannot help but note that **the Indian army,** as mentioned in the earlier section, **has at all times been following the orders of Back-Door British Maneuvered** Indian Politicians to defend **British-defined borders,** instead of taking it upon themselves to defend and protect critical centers of social, scientific and spiritual learning. **This is indicative of the dis-orientation in the Army's understanding of what its duty is.**

Generals of the Indian Army, Admirals, Commodores!! Are you aware that one of the key dimensions of the Strategic Defense Initiative required the reduction and degradation Indian Army from a of the formidable and feared fighting force, capable of protecting the country from any threat, into a degenerate, fourth-grade and politicized institution? As has been illustrated in the sections above, the widespread institutional failure has stemmed from the institutional leaders not understanding what their duty is, and being unable to involve with their Government for help to alter the situation, often not even knowing what question to ask.

Generals of the Indian army, Admirals, Commodores !! — who speak English and want documents to be translated into English, while each and every single one of their own Indian Jawans be they from Kashmir or from Kanyakumari speak fluent Hindi – just in case you do not know or realize, the word "**PRIVATIZATION**" is <u>NOT</u> an abbreviation for "**PRIVATE PARTS UNDER ELECTROCUTION**"; the pain in former case will be of a far more prolonged and far more severe intensity. From the bottom of our hearts and from the depths of our minds, we urge you at all costs to avoid this situation .....Quite frankly, we are already scared that you may soon not have your Private Parts anymore...oh no, nO, NO!!!!!....it is certainly not our implication that our Western-Brethen (aka the Pakistanis) plan to cut them off..............rather, **it is precisely our case that Your own Government,** whose orders you are duty-bound to unquestioningly follow, **has before the Supreme Court questioned Article 21 on the right of Indian Citizens to Privacy,** thus declaring that **these may no longer be** your "Private" Parts.

So just WHAT exactly do you propose to do? Well, whatever you choose to do, rest assured that we will be watching!!!! Should you need any help either way, do let us know.

Generals, Admiral and Commodores, Do you now understand the meaning of the doctrine stemming from the Strategic Defense Initiative: "reduce and downgrade the Indian Army to a degenerate, fourth-rate and politicized organization?" While we do not wish this state come to pass, the events are pointing in this direction. We urge the armed forces, as we urge all the other institutions of higher learning in the country to start re-examining the question of duty. As we have emphasized earlier, this is only understood in the context of History, Space and Time. If we keep ignoring this study, our fate is in the direction outlined above.

By the way how many in India know that the name "Syria" is a Latin-corrupted usage of the country called Surya by every Englishman, Arab and non-Arab alike – giving **therefore the Syrians/Suryans a far deeper anchor to Kashmir than most Indians realize, given that Kashmir is the Surya-Kshetra. How many Indians know that 12 massive temple complexes dedicated to the 12 aspects of the Surya, the Sun, were carefully laid in ruins over the last 200 years?**

Strangely, instead of talking to the Syrians, our Prime Ministers, Foreign Ministers and their spokespersons are more interested to sit-eat-dine with Kings of Saudi, Sultans of Gulf-States ....who at the first instance were themselves the funders of the Jihadi problem in Central Asia both in Syria and in Kashmir, through their proxy Pakistanis....or sit with the Portuguese who at the first available opportunity will revive their tradition of loot, plunder and pillage.

We started this article with the Spokesperson of our National Ruling Party saying that going forward India must look East, on the grounds that Hillary Clinton said so.

May, we please bring to the notice of our readers that the **Abbasid Caliph Haroon-Al-Rashid** had in accord with the Quranic injunction of the Prophet Muhammed (PBUH) issued a **dikkat to all devout Muslims to look East towards India** for knowledge and for a solution to their problems. **Of course, the Syrians also looked East.** They had made a number of appeals to the supposedly sane and intelligent Indians following the Haroon-Al-Rashid dikkat stemming from the Quranic Injunction to look East, particularly to India for help.....but in vain.

The Suryans/Syrians did attempt a solution to their problem looking East alright, — but it was minus India.

"India should look East" Indeed!! Parroting the Hillary Clinton's "Look East Policy" which was devised by the Americans to occupy, divide and destroy the Asian countries, has only proved that India is now delirious and Death may be soon to follow. Already we see the vultures landing on India, waiting to feed on its dead corpse, and we have already started selling its flesh at a hefty discount.

To what depths of shamelessness have we reached!

Appendix: From Anatolia To India – The Turkish Coup: Beginning Of The End Of Great Game

For more than 2000 years a war is being waged for the control of India and the access routes connected to it. The Turkey Coup is the beginning of the end of the Great Game, as it is known.

A gift from one crumbling Superpower
to a Rising Superpower:
But then why should India burn??
HAYATTA EN HAKIKI MURSIT ILIMDIR : THE TRUEST GUIDE IN
LIFE IS SCIENCE
– KEMAL ATATURK

History: From Ottoman Empire to today's Quagmire

Ancient Indian trade while centered in Kabul, spanned all the way outwards to Central Asia, thence Northwards to Russia and Westwards through Teheran, Baghdad, Damascus, Istanbul into the European heartland. Well established trade routes and the Merchants frequenting them were assured security by every kingdom, whether Indian or Iranian or Ottoman, no matter the other politics. Continuity of trade from India, China or Russia was thus ensured, with Europeans too using this route to enter India — the prized destination.

What is modern day Turkey was then perhaps the heart of the Sunni, Non-Arab and secularly-administered Ottoman Empire- which at its height which would stretch all the way from the Caucasus down to Arabian Peninsula, Iraq, most of Egypt, Northern coast of Africa and into the European Balkans. Damascus, in modern day Syria, was the primary center for Ottoman military and diplomatic rule from where they controlled all of Arabia and the northern strip of Africa and what is today's Middle East.

Critically it controlled the gateways from Europe to India — at least starting from the Ottoman conquest of Constantinople (in 1453 during the 2nd or 3rd Crusade-depending on how one counts – by the very young Sultan Mehmet II). The only other alternative route to connect India with Europe would be via Russia, but this route could not be opened up due to the conflict between the Eastern and the Western churches. Thus, then, all approaches from Asia to Europe were firmly under Ottoman control and with the rise of this non-Arab, Sunni, secular Caliphate, there ensued a 700-year era of restive peace, prosperity and development spanning the Middle East, Central Asia, China.

But other than Trade, there was an additional dimension — It would also serve as a flash point of three different religious groups: The Orthodox Church (First the Greek, then the Russian), next Islam – and with claims by both of these being seen as invalid by the more remote Vatican on its way to the holy land. The geophysical province of modern-day Turkey, properly called Anatolia, would at some point in history be under complete Orthodox Byzantine control and at some other points (most of subsequent history) under Islamic/Secular Ottoman control. Like-wise as the Ottomans pushed into Europe, vast parts of the Balkans would be at some point in history under Ottoman control and at other points (most of subsequent history) under Christian control. This Ottoman push into the Balkans, as well as their checkmating of the West in terms of the land route to India, has resulted in an animosity towards the Ottoman from both Russia and the West.

This triangular conflict carried on over the next 700 years vis-a-vis the Ottoman, although the rest of the Central Asia, East Asia and China had relative peace- with the Turks bearing the major brunt. Sometimes the West and Russia joined to fight the Ottomans/Turkey, sometimes Russia joined the Ottomans to fight the West, sometimes the West joined the Ottomans to fight Russia (instigate and support the Orthodox Greeks to fight the Turks, instigate and support the Turks to fight the Orthodox Russians, Instigate the Egyptians to fight the Turks, support first the former, then switching sides to the latter etc. Etc. according to the convenience of Mr. Palmerston, who by the way was also responsible for the forcible drugging of the Chinese using opium grown in India and for causing the first and second opium wars!!). And at other times Both Russia and Britain allied with the Ottomans to fight a third enemy e.g. the French Napoleon in the Egypt and Syrian invasions. And yet again Britain and France allied up to support Italian invasion of the Ottoman provinces of Tripolitana. Interesting also to note that the British rule in India had propagated the view that the Ottoman Sultan (at least from 1789 Selim III to the final nominal Sultan Abdülmecid 1924) was the Caliph of Pan-Islam and the Sultan in turn returned the British favor by issuing diktats to the Indian Muslims of India telling them to support British rule — But it is these same British who would later on push the case that it is not the Turks, but the Arabs who are the true Guardians of Islam!! What we hear in India is very different from what we hear in the rest of the World!!

This triangular fighting maintained some sort of a balance of power which finally was disrupted during the First World War and with discovery of oil in the Middle East and the breakdown of the Ottoman Empire. But until then, as long as the balance was reasonable, this geographical control of centrality in the only feasible trade routes, resulted in an enviable prosperity for both the Anatolian and Balkan halves of the Ottoman Empire. Now if the Western Europeans could find a way to circumvent this route, both Anatolia and the Balkans (viewing the latter as either under Islamic or under Orthodox rule – both being on the hostile radar of the West) would lose out and Western Europe would be the ascending power. Essentially from a religious basis on which these wars are fought, the Catholic & Protestant side would rise while the Orthodox Church and Islam would fall. Thus the intense and inherent dislike between Europeans and Ottomans, based on a Racial & Economical edifice and manifesting in Religions- sitting on two clashing expansionist empires, would lead to a strong resolve by the Europeans to try to undermine the Ottomans.

This prompted a West European scramble with Portuguese and the Spanish searching for sea routes to India, plundering Africa and America in the process. Interestingly according to their documents regarding the Treaty of Tordesillas, India is still considered their colony. We draw the attention of our reader to the recent visit of a senior Indian Minister (reader, find out his name!!) to Portugal in the fashion of a dedicated colonist-stooge, and inviting them back to India under the guise of "Portugal's World Class Competencies"!!!. The rise of this sea-based trade would result in the downfall of both Turkey and Byzantium. Anatolia and the Balkan region in general and Ottoman Turkey in particular would then change from being a highly prosperous zone to being the sick man of Europe—going significantly downwards after European ideological re-unification via the Treaty of Westphalia culminating in the World War -1 break-up the Ottoman Empire. As will be elaborated in the later part of this article, what we see in the region today is essentially an attempt by the counter-forces to reverse this situation (excepting that it is not Byzantium, but Russia, both of which are Orthodox).

And once the sea route to India was discovered, the Western Europeans (Catholics and England) made a determined attempt to disrupt and destroy the land route to India, which was now no longer necessary for them anyway. To this end they propped-up, instigated and fanned every possible sectarian, tribal and linguistic tension over the entire south-eastern part of the Eurasian landmass. This saw the creation of artificial nation states, with boundaries drawn in a manner as to create conflict, and which were perpetually ruled by thugs and stooges from tribes most favored by the West – the rule was perpetuated in a tyrannical manner. These artificially created nation-states, with ridiculously illogical borders, have become permanent impediments for the re-setting of the land route to India, thus permanently blocking what were once commercial and economic and spiritual highways connecting from Kashi, Agra, Kabul, via Isfahan, Teheran, Bagdad, Damascus and Syria to Ankara all the way into the European Union.

In each of these artificially-constructed tribal states, a pretension was made of merging or imposing the tribal beliefs into forms of Islam in a highly confused manner, as would suit the agenda of the West. This ensured that no native of the region would understand the geographic reality he was living in, nor would he understand the religion he was expected to follow, nor the reason for the death sentence handed down to him! (We ask our reader to ponder on whether the current Indian state has not been created in a similar manner, excepting that instead of imposing a confused Islam, it is a confused "Hinduism" super-imposed on an equally confused "Secularism." With this confusion after the introduction of this hitherto unknown "religion" and with an artificial language imposed on the name, which the oppressed Indians themselves converted into a Sanskritized form, we have forgotten what actually we were called, what we actually practiced and aimed for, and for what many Kings went to war, what value system they defended at the cost of their lives—all this is now lost into the oblivion.)

With the injection of oil money into this highly schizoid situation, treacherously competing tribal Monarchies were set up to ruthlessly suppress the populations and exploit the natural resources for use by the West. By default all these monarchies were pitted against the broken Ottoman Empire. Each Kingdom put to fight with all its neighbors...giving an endless series of chances to the West to pick and choose the Kingdoms according to West's ever changing definition of friend and enemies.

The Creation of Modern-day Turkey

With the defeat of the Central Forces and the Ottoman Empire and the Turkish debacle on the Russian front in World War 1, the British proceeded to implement this agenda on the Anatolian landmass in particular, after first splitting up the Ottoman Empire. The British aim was to break up the Ottoman by creating and supporting rebellions in each of the Ottoman governorates, separate them from the Ottomans and then subsequently break up the governorates and put arbitrary kingdoms with multi-ethnic factions, each under a British-chosen Sultan.

A critical approach for this destruction was to promise petty Arab chieftains ruler-ship of the entire territory after they won the war, if they went along with the British against the Ottoman Sultan — only to later deceive them. On the Armenian side, the Armenian genocide — which could be seen as the starting point of the Anatolian Breakup — was engineered by the Bad-Cop-British-instigated Sultan to clear Turkish lands out of infidels, an action not in consonance at all with the general history and culture of Turkey. Then they (the Good-Cop-Americans!!) shouted "We have to intervene!". At this same point in time, the Treaty of Sevres, primarily from Woodrow Wilson's viewpoint, envisaged the creation of both an Armenian and a Kurdish homeland, sowing the seeds for future conflicts. The Sultan Mehmed VI who was put in Turkey moved so as to make it an extremist-Sunni state which would then be anti-Shia, and who was helped by and helped the British to do this, was overthrown by General Mustafa Kemal Pasha and Turkey was brought to a more neutral configuration. Subsequently, in the Arab context, the British would renege on the Hussein–McMahon agreements cheating out the Arabs, implementing instead the agreements made by Mr. Sykes and Mr. Picot—neither of whom were Arabs. Indians to note that this is the same Henry McMahon of Partitioners Inc.!! Why then do we still view the McMahon Line as valid? What mistakes did the Arabs commit? What did the British do to the Arabs? Why do Indians still trust the British after this history?

The Turkish state however differed from the other kingdoms of North Africa, Arabia and Central Asia in that they were the seat of a very large vibrant and dynamic Empire that had lasted several centuries, that had fought several wars with the Europeans and which had imbibed good army training from them. Although by the start of the twentieth century it was not in the best of shapes, they were nevertheless able to mount a resistance to the designs of British and their allies. This resistance was the Turkish Independence Movement which overthrew the Sultan Mehmed VI who was in accordance with the allied design deviating from the established principles of the Ottoman Empire and was moving under British orders to towards Islamic fundamentalism—a process already set in motion by Sultan of the Ottomans Abdul Hamid II.

The Turkish Independence Movement was able to a definite extent able to check mate the European objective of the complete fragmentation of the Ottoman Empire, and succeeded in keeping its heartland, Anatolia, free from European administration (having repudiated the Treaty of Sevres) and establishing firm Turkish rule under the subsequent treaty of Lausanne (1923). The Anglo-American objectives in this regard are clear from the Treaty of Sevres, which they tried to enforce: to keep the area fragmented under Kurds, Greeks, Armenians, and Muslims each protected by a combination of various European countries. But this, as stated above, the leadership of the Turkish Independence Movement was able to avoid under the leadership of Mustafa Kemal Ataturk, the hero of Gallipoli.

So then, while at a time most of the other parts of the Ottoman Empire, Central Asia, North Africa were under the rule of British-installed puppet Kings, the Turks were able to have a strong Nationalist rule in their homeland. Although, it is noteworthy that Kemal Ataturk accepted the reality of downsizing of the Ottoman Empire's burdens of the Middle Eastern and Egyptian possessions (as the Soviet Union would downsize eighty years later to become Russia).

We should nevertheless note that the fissures which Ataturk was able to hold together, are precisely the points used to keep Turkey under blackmail on most policy issues today. Once in every two decades, the Kurdish question is raised, the Kurds are used for the work of the interests of the Anglo-American combine and then they are ditched again. Raising this bogey of the Kurdish issue has almost become like a golden rule in the geopolitics of the Middle East. (for the reader: What might be the implications of the recent opening of an Indian Consulate in Kurdistan?) Next, the threat of raising the question of the Armenians and the Armenian Genocide, which anyway has been instigated and mediated by the British themselves, is kept dangling – as is the question of the part of Cyprus that was disputed by the Ottomans and the Greeks.

This blackmail permitted Turkey to be used (at least to some extent) to manipulate the Arab politics till 1975, when the Americans figured out a better way to disrupt the Arab Politics by using Wahabism. Although the pressure on Turkey then decreased on this front, the Anglo-American combine still continued to meddle with the Turkish internal affairs, since they wanted to make it a vassal state similar to the other Arab states. This last context makes the current purge by carried out by Erdogan, very hard for the Anglo-American lobby to digest.

Let it also be remarked here that the failure of the Anglo-American combine to use Turkey to turn to fundamentalist Islam and push this virulent brand according to the Anglo-American interests would lead to the Anglo-American lobby to look elsewhere (Saudi Arabia) to get this job done for them. Thus, it is precisely this failure in Turkey that caused Saudi Arabia to turn to the extremist and virulent path. The consequent lessons for India should not be lost on us. If Pakistan were to refuse to allow extremist Islam, what might that mean in the light of this?

Amongst all the secular institutions set up by Kemal Pasha, the most noteworthy of these was the Turkish army, which has played a critical role in maintaining a healthy stability of the nation-state. The Turkish army has played a very critical role in keeping Turkey healthy. A noteworthy quote by a very senior Turkish General Cevik Bir (who played a very critical role and arrest in the 1997 Turkey coup and the control of the Islamic danger rising in Turkey): "In Turkey we have a marriage of Islam and democracy. (...) The child of this marriage is secularism. Now this child gets sick from time to time. The Turkish Armed Forces is the doctor which saves the child. Depending on how sick the kid is, we administer the necessary medicine to make sure the child recuperates". The army has seen to it that secular education is available for all children, they have seen to it that political parties pushing either radical Islamic or radical leftist views were outlawed, they have seen to it that the Tariqas (a multitude of Islamic Sufi orders which often get very cultish and are subject to infiltration by foreigners and undesirable elements) have been kept at a healthy balance, they have ensured that views are not enforced on specified minority religions (e.g. Orthodox Christians, Armenians and Jews, but many are not thus classified). The army frequently discharges officers who involve in radical Islamic movements. They have stepped in to force the government's hand during times of economic mismanagement and crisis.

The British in particular and the West in general, have since been continuously trying to meddle with this healthy and secular configuration and have attempted to establish their own rule via fundamentalists. At least four concerted attempts have been made in the post WW-II era so far – and in all these four attempts the Turks, with very high credit going to the Turkish Army were successfully able to thwart the designs of the British and their Western allies. Thus, then this realization put the destruction of the Turkish army at high priority on the agenda of the Anglo-American combine.

Smashing up of the South Central (Eur)asian landmass, the Arab reaction, counter-reactions and the Turkish overlook

And then following the Palmerston doctrine, the encirclement of each of the broken empires be it a friend or enemy, the view being contextual anyway, was set in motion around Turkey. As part of this ever-expanding Encirclement project territorial and other disputes with Bulgaria, Hungary and Romania and Syria and Iraq were raked up, the Armenian question being put in abeyance for blackmail. The Palmerston Doctrine was centered to deal with two primary targets: Mohammedans and the Russians which reverberated the age-old Catholic Rivalry of reformation and counter-reformation envisioning the destruction of Protestantism, Eastern Orthodoxy and Mohammedenism (Islam). Note also that this rivalry was a key motive in the creation of highly cultish Jesuit orders, which will link into both India and the Turkish question via Operation Gladio-B (see later in this article).

Palmerston argued that to do this, we side with one or the other depending upon our choice. They also created an astonishing definition of Moderates and Radicals, Secular and Religious—labels that could be seamlessly and interchangeably used on anyone and everyone in a manner that gives maximum benefit to the West. In order to have this seamless interchangeability, after the fall of the Ottoman Empire a final partition of Palestine was engineered to create the State of Israel, democratically (via voting in the UN) using the artificially-created Partition of India first, and creation of multiple republics in Indian subcontinent — which, like their Middle Eastern counterparts, have been fighting with one another since inception.

The ruthlessly-exploited-population of these alphanumeric nation-states created post the fall of the Ottoman Empire have reacted in two different ways: One mode was what we call now the Pan-Arabic Movement, which is the basis of the rise of the Baath Party. In the early stages, they were referred to as the Young Turks (in the context of the Turkish vicinity) because they followed Kemal Pasha. Nevertheless, it should be clearly understood by Indians that the word "Baath" is Renaissance – Renaissance

from the retrograde and interpretative forms of Islam being imposed on
the Arabs by the West in general and by the British in particular. They
deposed the British–appointed Monarchs and established secular-socialist
rule, retaining armed forces as a guarantee of secularism, perhaps in the
manner of Turkey. In the entire de-forked dominions of the erstwhile
Ottoman Empire this secularized-socialist replacement of the British-
puppet Monarchs occurred. Muammar Qaddafi, Gamel Nasser, Hafiz al
Assad, Saddam Hussein and Mohammed Mossadegh would be the new
leaders, keeping their countries for the people and by the people in the
half comprising of Libya, Egypt, Syria, Iraq and Iran. In the next round of
this continuous game, the West wanted to eliminate these secular-socialist
rulers who had deposed their pet-monarchs.

As a counter by the West to the secularization occurred in these
provinces, another mode of reaction was seen in the other half comprising
of Saudi-Arabia, Bahrain, Qatar. These were used by the West to start a
counter-reformation nurturing, reviving and rejuvenating extreme tribal
interpretations of Islam e.g. Wahabi(Arab), Salafi(Qatar), Hanofi (Syria)
'isms by endlessly creating multiple alphanumeric combinations of terrorist
outfits with the intention of battering the Secular Socialist Republics
mentioned in the previous paragraph.

When these terrorist outfits failed in this job, clandestine intelligence
agencies were used to eliminate the leaders and when that failed as well,
direct military intervention by the West was fostered in the name of
restoring democracy. The only mistake these socialist republics had
committed was that they distributed the natural resources and wealth of
their countries to their own populations, unlike the unquestionably-loyal
puppet-monarchs set up the British who sucked up every last pie from
their own people to flow into their colonial masters' accounts. The first
democratic secular republic to be replaced by covert operations was that
of the Iranian Government when democratically elected Mohammed
Mossadegh was removed by a CIA coup and the Shah Reza Pahlavi was
brought back to "rule" – read "to execute absolute plunder" — which then
led to the second stage and form resistance to the Western Hegemony – by
going back to the puritanical spiritual roots – in the case of Iran it was Shia
Islam.

The other countries of the first group (Libya, Egypt, Turkey, Syria, Iraq)
were not subjected to this second spiritual transition because they were
able to learn from the Mossadegh affair and were able to purge out the

divisive elements before the secular-socialist rule could be deposed. Unlike Mossadegh, they were able to continue the secular-socialist paradigm in their countries for over fifty years. Not only to merely continue to rule fairly to their own people, but they were also to mount a counter to the despotic Western-backed Monarchies like Kuwait, Qatar, Bahrain and Saudi Arabia and the influences emanating from them. The height their determination was perhaps seen in the Iraqi occupation of Kuwait which was stealing Iraqi oil by parallel digging, and fomenting trouble in all these secular republics using the backing of their Western masters. And at which point the West could take the affront to their hegemony no more — and decided upon the route of direct intervention to take Saddam Hussein out. Emboldened by their success in this operation, they then took Egypt's Mubarak out, following it up with taking Libya's Muammar Qaddafi out, and succeeding there as well, they now tried to take Syria's Bashar Assad out, but as of today have not been successful in this last one...nor were they successful in the near simultaneous attempt to take out Erdogan in Turkey, where the Ataturk was successful in purging divisive derisive elements and created a secular Turkish state— Actually, the latest Turkey coup attempt even at the outset looks like an absolutely ridiculous attempt, bordering on insanity, by generals who did not study even course – 101 of engineering a coup.

The Oil-Based Geopolitcs and the Energy Angle; Breaking the Syria-Iran-Russia Connection using Turkey

Six regime changes (Lebanon, Syria, Iran, Iraq, Turkey, and Russia and Ukraine) were planned during the Obama-administration, which were not directly linked to the Arab Spring. The motivation stemmed from agreements signed between Saudi-Arabia, Qatar, Bahrain and US to execute oil trading in a manner which could perhaps be summarized as: "US-In, Europe-Down, Russia-Out, Saudi Arabia-Up, Iran-Down". Under a ridiculous deal this agreement was reached between Kerry and Bandar Sultan, with the Saudis almost obsessively insisting that the Shia brand of Islam be completely eliminated and that they should have the complete control of the entire Islamic world. The former position pitted the Saudis against the Shias and the second position pitted Saudi with Turkey which is the de-facto leader of Sunni world and they made two types of enemies in the process. Perhaps, this agreement between Kerry and Bandar Sultan is very similar to the Hussein-McMahon agreement that was used to destroy the Ottomans. Will future historians write again about the Bandar-Kerry agreement as the earlier and current ones did about the Hussein-McMahon?

So as part of the deal Saudi Arabia would help in executing all the regime changes, if in return the Arabs were made the lords, or more precisely what they thought to be the lords, since in a similar game Saudi Arabia was given control of Mecca and Medina which post-1970 has been changed into a gigantic business enterprise in the name of Islamic Hajj and then used by the Americans anyway. In the current context, Saudi Arabia was convinced or forced to drop the price of oil, going against all OPEC considerations. It was calculated that in 2 years of this lowered-price-regime Russia and Syria will both crash as had happened in the 1986 collapse of the Soviet economy. When the demand for oil had gone up by 20 % the price dropped by 50 % – against all the laws of economics!! The Saudis had agreed to bear the losses for two years, until Syria could be taken over and then they could re-hike the price again.

This however was the miscalculation. The Russians had learnt valuable lessons from the 1986 crash which occurred in the Gorbachev and Yelstin era, and Russian exports had since been diversified heavily. Not only that, they also accumulated several tons of Gold, and were able to pull off trading in either the Euro or in the Rouble. The question of keeping Russia (the largest ONG producer) down was discussed earlier, and neither group in this alliance wanted the oil to be under Shia (Iranian) control. Thus sanctions were imposed on Iran, and to get them lifted Russia (note that European Diplomatic help would be on the same side of this paradigm) had to pressurize Iran to abandon its nuclear program.

In the immediate context of the Turkey coup, two competing projects aimed to reduce the Russian role in Europe's Energy dependency. One was a Iran–Iraq-Syria-Lebanon pipeline to Europe, projected as a purely Islamic – read "non-aligned"- pipeline. While an agreement towards this was signed in 2011 (which outraged the anti-Shia Saudi Arabs and sparking a local cry "Syria must Go"), Qatar approached Syria, and suggested they shelve this project, and implement instead a pipeline from its own North Field, transiting Saudi Arabia, Jordan via Syria all the way to Turkey, and onto the EU. Syria's Assad however rejected this suggestion, choosing instead to support former, finalizing the agreement with Iran and Iraq in 2012. Thus, while the ISIS and ISIL were instigated by their Western masters to destroy the Syrian refineries that would service this pipeline, Qatar took a deep vested interest in removing Assad....

This was done by raising the Shia-Sunni divide, but only this time Qatar-style by creating, nurturing and sponsoring the Al-Nusra front as an affiliate of the Saudi Arabian Al-Qaeda. The Saudis were enamored with ISIS/ISIL/Daesh mode because they carry the brand of Wahabbi islam. The extreme cruelties perpetuated by ISIS/ISIL/Daesh in terms of beheading children, women and any Muslim who was not a Wahabbi surpassed even the expectations of both their masters – The Saudis and the Americans, the latter referring to these groups as "Moderate"! But they were equally taken-aback by the strange other-worldly explanations offered when the ISIS and ISIL was beaten back and melted away with the determined response of Shiite Iran-Iraq-Syria-Lebanon axis, despite their demonstration of extreme inhuman cruelty during the course of the war.

This left the battle on the ground in the hands of the Al-Nusra front – which recently morphed into Jabhat-Fateh-Al-Sham, prophetically stating that they are severing all links with Al-Qaeda — a wish that was instantly granted by the Al-Qaeda leadership. Thus transformed the demoniac, barbarian Al-Nusra Front into the American definition of "Moderate". The Al-Nusra Front surpassed in ability most of the groups created earlier and was actually the diamond tip of the spear used in the attack on Syria, with extensive core and advanced level training being provided by veterans in Pakistan. Indians should take critical note of the role of Pakistan as a staging post for the International game. If Pakistan were not separated from India, would the West have been able to play this game? If Pakistan was not fighting with Afghanistan and there were no internal rebellions raked up in Balochistan would the West have been able to play this game? Do we, the Indians, see now at least one of the long-term consequences of the Partition of India? Alas, we are taught that it is meaningless to "try to re-play history".

In addition to the geopolitics of Syria, which has long been known to have a critical location as a transit corridor, in the pipelines originating and terminating in other countries, the discovery of extremely vast energy-resources in both on the mainland of the Syrian territory and in the Mediterranean Sea between Syria and Cyprus, caused matters to take a far more serious turn. British and American strategists began to view this as a way to pull Europe off the Russian dependence with for example a 2014 US army SSI report explicitly saying "US-led military intervention has a key role to play in managing conflicts and tensions in the Eastern Mediterranean, especially the prospect of Syria destabilising into de facto civil war". More complicating is the aspect that the zones which

contain these vast natural resources do not recognize man-made
boundaries, and are overlapping between Syria and several neighboring
nations (Israel, Greece, Cyprus etc), the potential for future conflict is 100%
realizable. Thus, the dismemberment of Syria has been one of the geo-
strategic aims of the British-American combine, and is supported in this
regard by Syria's neighbors, including Israel.

We mention here that with the descent of Syria into the civil-war (read
foreign sponsored mayhem), the creation of a very prosperous state based
on transshipment economy and on its own vast natural reserves has been
impossible to so far accomplish, the Islamic pipeline (from Iran) is not
completed as scheduled.

The British-American interests have thus attempted to push Assad into
accommodating the Western interests or face the threat of being re-placed
with a combination of rebel forces backed by Qatar and the other Gulf
states, the ISIS and Turkey, which will then push for the dismemberment of
Syria.

Critical then in this Western Geo-strategy, was Turkey's role in the
destabilization of Syria. Once the Turks are controlled, the regime change
in Syria can then be executed via ground forces provided by Turkey, and
the oil can be piped to Europe at a price convenient to the Anglo-American
interests. They forced Turkey to set up training bases for IS/Daesh, ISIL
etc, — for implementing which the Americans needed good interaction with
the Turkish army's command. The American penetration of the Turkish
Armed forces, using Fethullah Gulen's organization, came into play. While
working with Erdogan, they also established and maintained inside Turkey
a parallel structure, so that if Erdogan were to subsequently refuse to toe
the US line, as in-fact he did, they could fall back on this parallel mode. This
game however angered the Turkish Nationalist Establishment, adding fuel
to which was the American funding of the Kurds. In a sense, it would be fair
to say, that the Americans before executing the Turkey coup over-estimated
their own abilities inside Turkey and perhaps erroneously assumed that
Turkish Nationalists had been heavily bought out (via for example Colonel
Campbell's Nigerian-Bank affair).

Nevertheless, as explained earlier, Western motives for their Turkey
policy is intended to control both Russia in the North as well as to serve as a
tool to control Arab politics in the South. The centuries old Russo-Turkish
antagonism was exploited by America to pull Turkey into its fold, and
Turkey then became a pivot in this game. By becoming a NATO member,

Turkey (inadvertently??) got pulled into all these conflicts while the series
of historical battles between Turkey and Orthodox Russia was now viewed
through the Cold War paradigm.

As at the height of the Cold War the artificially constructed nation-
state of Afghanistan would be the staging/learning and training ground
the Mujaheddin to overthrow Russians from Afghanistan, so too would
all similarities carry over to later training of the Chechens were trained
after the collapse of the Soviet Union. This training whose ideological and
informational backbone was provided by the West, was facilitated by
Turkey, financed by Saudi Arabia (Wahabbi Islam), Qatar (Salafi Islam) etc.
And so in this context Turkey became their friend.

To keep Turkey in their hold, they had agreed to Turkish possessions
in Cyprus, ignore the Armenian genocide, and ignore the Kurdish question
and respect the territorial integrity of Turkey. But as an unexpected side-
effect, in the name of fighting the Cold War anyone who claimed to be an
enemy of the Russians were trained to fight (with Russia from the American
perspective, but having their own complex set of motives). Fortunately
or unfortunately, the people who answered this call-to-arms by the West
were the poor and secular Muslims from the erstwhile Soviet republics
and if their numbers fell short and another endless number was provided
from much poorer African (Ethiopia, Somalia, Sudan, Nigeria) and far-East
Asian republics (Philippines, Indonesia, Malaysia) and from the crown jewel
of the colonial empire: Indian Subcontinent Muslims (India, Bangladesh,
Pakistan, Myanmar); this last being our domain of responsibility.

Thus, while from the viewpoint of the Cold-War the training that was
provided by the Americans, facilitated by Turkey and financed by the Arabs,
was viewed as the American encircle-Russia agenda, the Turks could well
have seen the matter differently. What externally appeared as the breakup
of the Soviet Union, a historical event which occurred at this juncture in
time, gave the Turks the impression that they could settle their 900-year old
score with the Russians.

Except in the case of Taliban and Afghan Mujahedin, most of the
training for the other groups was facilitated by the Turkish Army. This had
very serious consequences in the question of the stability and historical
basis of Turkey. The last two decades worth of interaction of certain
sections of the army officers who were assigned for training these groups
in collaboration with the West, led to a drastic change in the most sacred
institution setup by the Ataturk: the Turkish Army. Most of the

coordination and supervision of these groups was assigned to the Turkish Second Army which operated around Incirlik and other nearby bases. Coincidentally or accidentally (read: by design !!) most of the plotters, planners and executors of the current Turkey Coup who were all booked under sedition cases following the failed Turkey coup, belonged to this particular batch of the Turkish army.

Ahmed Davutoglu (former PM of Turkey) was an American choice and was funded by the Saudis and the Salafi and pushed a very pro-Sunni Wahabbi stance and anti-Shia stance....which was not the hallmark of the Turkish stand. On the Syrian question, when Erdogan was making statements that it is good to have Assad as part of a transitional government, Davutoglu had made statements against Assad. He had turned a blind eye and also actively encouraged the arming of the Kurds. He also masked American-led training for the terrorists, with all moves that were dangerous to Turkey as being exclusively anti-Russia, and this permitted further penetration into the army. A good amount of the blame for the recent fall of Turkey into this quagmire could perhaps rest on him, which is why Erdogan relieved him of Prime Ministership. This is another reason why Turkey is purging so many people who have caused Turkey to deviate from the healthy policy. Most of the Turkey coup participants were trained as NATO's re-deployment force. Austrian and German sources estimate that 60% of the police and 70 % of the civil administration and 20 % of the armed forces were penetrated by the pro-American Fethullah Gulen followers. Those who penetrated the Civil Services and Judiciary further helped with the cover up of the true aim of this operation. Do we see any signs of a similar cover up in India as well?

As mentioned earlier, a critical step in the engineering of the Turkey coup was to pull Fethullah Gulen to America and use his organization to infiltrate the entire Turkish establishment – not just the army. More revealingly the Fethullah Gulen Network has spread its network into the Judiciary, Police, Academicians and Border Patrol Units. Right now the Turkish Intelligence is tracking and tracing and most of these Turkey coup plotters supporters and financier inside Turkey escaping under ISIS/ISIL/ DAESH/ PKK / Moderate Western backed terrorist groups operating on the Turkish border. Some of them have been nabbed by the Turkish intelligence before they crossed the border and some are nabbed inside the Terrorist controlled cities themselves.

As a historical note, we should mention the 1807 Janissary Coup (Sultan's elite bodyguards) had assassinated Sultan Selim III who was modernizing the army heavily, and then again they would force the subsequent Sultan Mahmud under threat of death to call off the Modernization of the Army. Mahmud II would in the famous 1826 "Auspicious Incident" execute over 6000 of them (due to a coup which they either staged or were caused to stage) and abolish the order entirely. The Janissaries had a tight link with the Bektashi religious order and this relationship played a critical role in the decision of the Ottoman administration to decide to end the Janissaries. The outlawing of the Bektashi has resulted in its re-manifestation and the formation of the Nakshbandi from where descends Said Nursi, under whom Fethullah Gulen manifests. The historical continuity should now be obvious.

Indians should note that this is precisely the danger of de-criminalizing the likes of Abhinav Bharat and propping up similar individuals and organizations, as well as of the multitude of decadent spiritual charlatans Sri, Sri-squared, Sri-cubed, varieties of Anandas (Nityanandas and Vivekanandas of all hues), Doctorjis, Gurujis, Panditjis, Matajis etc. India should take a good lesson from the Bektashi question mentioned above. It also has a critical bearing on the elimination of Hemant Karkare. We shall also examine these issues in more detail below.

Fethullah Gulen has been courted by the American Administration since 1971, as part of Operation Gladio-B, which mediates the NATO's collaboration with radical Islam. (For more on Operation Gladio-B, see the article in this journal on Kashmir.) The Americans wanted to install in Turkey a rule similar to what was achieved in Egypt (Sadat who patched up with Israel and who was completely pro-American). But as elaborated earlier, the Turkish had their own agenda, and again, too weak a Turkey would not be able to fulfill the American aim of controlling the Arabs. The Turks were no fools however, and although as part of the role played by Turkey in Operation Gladio – B, they had to take in the radical Islamic elements under the Encircle-Russia objective, they were able to not only get what they wanted in a return bargain, but were also able to ensure that these terrorist elements would always remain under their control. The Americans soon realized that handling the Turkish Army or the Turkish Politicians is not a cakewalk, so the penetration via the Gulen movement into the Turkish Civil Society, in addition to the Army was pushed forward with far greater vigor. Also noteworthy is that with the fall of the Islamic Brotherhood and the Morsi government in Egypt, most of the cadre relocated to Turkey and further helped penetrate into Turkish civil society and Army. No matter what name these groups carry and what flavour is attributed to them, they started meddling towards the transformation of Turkish society into a rock solid image of the Wahabi brand of Islam...convenient to both British-America and Saudi Arabia.

The Turkish president realized that, contrary to any indications to the contrary, the Americans are bent on creating a Kurdish state. Indeed, he has seen them being armed from Mosul to Syria in the name of fighting the ISIS, which the Americans themselves had created. But he correctly recognized that these will be used to fight against Turkey as well, certainly when not being used in the anti-Russia campaign. This is somewhat similar to the situation we have in Kashmir where Americans trained Taliban, Mujahedin, LeT, etc with the objective of fighting the Russians, but these got pushed over to India.

But when the Americans finally concluded that Erdogan had his own agenda and was not going to play their game, they decided to try to take him out and put someone else and thus complete the fourth regime change agenda, and this now became a high priority for the Obama administration.

They staged a massive incident by shooting down the Russian plane. This alarmed the Russians who then got their ELINT to monitor Turkey in a 24/7 mode. Once the Russian ELINT started monitoring the Turkish communications, they picked up the existence of the danger of a Turkey coup, involving NATO-trained rapid re-deployment forces who were using a WhatsApp common group to plan a Turkey coup. The Russians at this point did not speak a word except to shut down Russian tourist traffic to and from Turkey. With the magnitude of the Turkey coup becoming clear, they realized that Turkey will become another Libya or Iraq and face a very grave danger of being further partitioned, in the manner of the failed Sevres Treaty, and that this would be followed by a partition of Syria as well. The Russians also realized that if a hard-line Sunni party came to power in Turkey, these hard-line Jihadists would enter Russia, complicating further the current problems is Ukraine. The danger of allowing the Turkey coup to go through was far too high.

Shortly before the actual Turkey coup was to take place, the Russians had presented the evidence to Erdogan, to prove the American backing. Interestingly, the moment the Turkey coup started, the NBC reported that Erdogan has fled into Germany—thereby hoping to destroy the morale of his followers and lure them into meekly surrendering to the Turkey coup plotters. While NBC claimed that they got this information from an unnamed military source, the Turkish sources realized that it is General Campbell who pushed this. This clearly showed that NBC was acting at the behest of a high level international group that planned the Turkey coup.

Not only did the Russians warn Erdogan, but their Spetsnaz forces were actually following him. The Presidential jet was escorted by two or three fighter jets loyal to him. On their way back from the Marmaris resort, F-16s coming in from Incirlik locked into not only onto Erdogan's plane, but also onto his loyal escorting F-16's . At this highly critical juncture, the Russian president, Putin himself stepped in and issued a straight warning to the Americans that he would within the next 120 seconds activate the S-500 missiles and shoot every NATO plane in the sky within a 500 km range. The threatening F-16 planes (not inexplicably as commonly thought now??) backed off and did not return to base in Incirlik, but flew onto Greece where they sought asylum. On a side-note, the Turkish Government is threatening legal recourse against NBC for propagating false information, asking them as to how they found that Erdogan is fleeing Turkey and heading out to Germany.

When the Turkey coup was in progress, the President called upon the Turkish people to come out to the streets to make sure the Turkey coup fails. Strangely, the only ones to answer this call, at least in the initial phase, were the Muslim extremist elements inside Turkey. These would have sided with the Turkey coup-plotters—but when they realized it is going to fail, they pretended to switch sides to move the culpability away from the US involvement, because both the Turkey coup-plotters and the extreme radical elements were funded by Saudi-Qatar-CIA-Fethullah Gulen combine.

This is the existential danger that Turkey faced and as the last and only resort made a 180-degree-U-turn away from West, NATO and US, and away from the marauding Saudi brand of Islamic groups (as practiced by the compliant monarchies) and gravitated towards Russia and Iranian viewpoint.

That is why when Erdogan successfully returned he decided to purge Turkey of this infiltration completely in a legal manner, after a fair trial. If he does this, 21 years of penetration effort will be lost to the West, which is now shouting itself hoarse —- losing Turkey for them means losing Syria.....and a lot more!

Forgetting about any international geo-political lessons, the minimum the Turks learnt was that the West wanted to further fragment the Ottoman Empire; and by harboring these terrorists at the behest of the Westerners to fulfill their objectives has corrupted Turkey's secular military institution itself. Academicians, lawyers, administrators etc became one with the terrorists and propelled Turkey in the direction of the failed state of Pakistan. Exactly then our Western neighbor aka Pakistan is a sense exact mirror image of Turkey – minus the good assistance of Kemal Pasha at its founding, minus the knowledge and wisdom acquired from centuries of existence as an Empire, minus the strong secular army, minus the leadership of Erdogan.

Turkey Coup: The Implications for India

However, the massive purge instituted by the Turkish President may well be successful in preventing the Definitely Assured Destruction of Turkey and this is precisely what the Turkish Foreign Minister is warning India. That India will now be the staging ground for training various terrorist factions, which may lead to the same situation as occurred in Turkey as well as counter-right wing radical elements (Operation Gladio-B in the Indian context) taking roots. Even if the terrorists that India is told to harbor or otherwise assist are of an anti-Pakistan or anti-Islamic nature, India would do well to avoid finding itself in the same danger that Turkey did.

Firstly, Indians should learn from the Turkish example of the Bektashi orders, the danger of de-criminalizing the likes of Abhinav Bharat and propping up similar individuals and organizations, as well as of the multitude of decadent spiritual charlatans Sri, Sri-squared, Sri-cubed, varieties of Anandas (Nityanandas and Vivekanandas of all hues), Doctorjis, Gurujis, Panditjis, Matajis etc. Because of the complete absence of scientific standards, and the brain-numbing devotion expected from the members, these organizations and extremely susceptible to infiltration and foreign control, the yoga or the meditation etc being the garb.

In addition to the question of international terrorism and its role in the turmoil of nation-states, there is also the second very critical dimension of radical internal changes to the main body of the country's society via the Fethullah Gulen and associated organizations. This was the second (and perhaps far more serious!!) existential danger realized by Turkey. In the context of India, Hemant Karkare had compiled a report extent several thousand pages on this deep penetration into India as well, which today our Ministers have got classified and do not want the people of India to know. This will be discussed in a later issue of this journal.

This is the context of the warning given by the Turkish Ambassador and by the Turkish Foreign Minister to India, which we should take with extreme seriousness, because Turkey itself was nearly taken over by US-sponsored Saudi brand of terrorism. True it is that this brand of Terrorism will be anyway opposed and possibly wiped out by the Ankara-Teheran-Baghdad-Beirut-Moscow axis, but in the process the hydra will spill over to other nations especially into India, into Balochistan the no-man's land, into Afghanistan and into Baltistan. Then on it will be fully utilized by our Western neighbor to disrupt, destroy, destabilize the Republic of India starting with Kashmir; and there is always a good possibility that this Hydra will morph itself as Balochistan- or Baltistan- freedom fighters and will get all their support to re-invigorate themselves – paradoxically from India itself!! Only to destroy India first and then strike straight at Iran, Iraq, Syria and Turkey from the backdoor, in consonance with the geopolitical aims of their highest masters.

Naively it looks like India is falling in the trap psychotically thinking that this step will contain our Western neighbor and bring some peace to Kashmir, whereas in-fact the actual danger would be of our losing Kashmir altogether. We will be following the same trap that was laid for Turkey...by training various groups to de-stabilize Syria etc. as most of these groups are trained with the ultimate aim of destabilizing Russia, their masters will turn a double-blind-eye and triple-deaf-ears when the Republic of India burns under their onslaught. It would be like four-dimensional chessboard played by sixteen players with no rules whatsoever.

The Saudis have sensed the American sense of defeat and abandonment in the Turkish and now the Syrian affair, are meanwhile pushing into Pakistan and signing military-deals, and making it into a Wahabbi state. This will have disastrous consequences for the sub-continent. While the Pakistan-China axis will be used to batter India and the Saudi-Pakistani axis will be used to batter Iran.

And even if neither of these approaches to hit Iran work, at the very least ISIS fighters fleeing the Middle Eastern/Central Asian theater will be planted into Balochistan and Baltistan, not to mention other soft Indian cities. The tech-savvy ISIS who were trained by the Americans to fight the Russians, who are using remote controlled machine guns, RPGs, mortars that can be operated via a laptop or mobile phone and other high-end technology will be surprised to see that the Indian army (which is a regional power, 4th largest in world!!!!) which upon waking up to this 5th generation technological war has only recently started laying fiber optic cables for controlling command structures in Ladakh and Leh, a step taken by Iraq 30 years ago, but yet has today became a failed and divided state.

The Saudis will dump arms which they purchased from China into Balochistan, while arms which they purchase from the Americans will be dumped into Pakistan. The self-styled Turbaned Anarchy – Islamic State by ISIS "Caliphate" (which is neither a state nor has anything to do with Islam!!!), that is battered up and has been battered up the Central Eurasia theater, will be re-located to Balochistan or Afghanistan. From there they will again return to the age-old problem of battering Iran and Russia. Depending upon American Internal Governmental Policies post Trump election, the CIA could well bypass their own government (as they have done several times before) and dump the job of training these Balochistan-based terrorists onto India citing India's "Regional Power Status" —- a status which is caricatured by pragmatic capitalists of the Anglo-American enterprises and recognized only by self-delusory Indian leaders of all shades, not to mention the bottle-fed corporate-media and IT "Czars" of India Inc.

While we recognize that the borders between India, Pakistan and Afghanistan are completely illogical drawn so as to serve the interests of the West, and need not be recognized as valid, let Indians clearly understand that any form of terrorism based in Balochistan would be primarily directed at hitting the Iranian underbelly, it is not intended to help India by breaking-up its "arch-rival" Pakistan per-se, in the fashion of the wishful thinking of the "emotional idiots" who were hurt by the Partition. Even if from the viewpoint of our immediate vicinity, it appears to be in our self-interest, should India support this?? If your answer is simply "yes", we urge you to read this entire article once and once again.

What conclusions should we draw from the Pakistani accusation, made with the arrest of Kulbhushan Yadav, that India has been involved in setting up the DAESH in Pakistan and the EU reports that US, Turkey and India and Brazil are the main suppliers of weapon components to the DAESH? While both of these allegations are completely bogus and devoid of logical basis (don't the EU members themselves sell arms on both sides of a conflict regardless of morals), the question as to their timing suggests that we are being setup for the next move. This will be discussed in a later article.

The American shielding of Fethullah Gulen using the mind-numbing logic that he has not committed any crimes in America or the grounds of un-obtainable proof of his direct involvement or intentions to commit atrocities against Turkey is similar to the mind-numbing logic which Britain has used on the Government of India when we requested the extradition of every known terrorist leader residing in Britain. Unsurprisingly or surprisingly (depending upon the IQ of our reader!!) the current Indian Government is using the same logic to refusing the extradition request of the Fethullah Gulen followers as requested by Turkey. Yet we demand the extradition of Dawood Ibrahim (while conveniently excluding Riyaz Bhaktal the founder of Indian Mujaheddin, and Shafi Armar, the founder of the Indian branch of ISIS known as IUT). What is worse, certain sections in India seem to be keen on setting up similar kind of training bases for Balochistan and Baltistan and Kurdistan (!!!!) while the correct thing for us to do would instead be to focus on shutting down the existing terrorist camps inside Pakistan using all available non-diplomatic routes.

Does the Turkish ambassador's and the Foreign Minister's warning to India now make sense? (Again more recently Erdogan himself warned Modi.) Does the Indian stand on this request resonate with the reply of the Americans to the Indian communication regarding a RAW Joint Secretary who has defected over to the US....."who?"..."we don't know his address"..."what wrong has he done?" ...... "details of our processes are not public"......

When the RAW counter intelligence was going to arrest this traitor and defector, the PMO's office and the Home Ministry pushed them go slow, and gave him a window of 24 hours to escape to Nepal and from there to the US. Contrary to the standard CIA policy of disowning assets, he was fully assisted in his escape to the US by the CIA, risking an exposure of their role. Having him under Indian interrogation would have risked far more than mere CIA's hand being exposed, for he was only a conduit for a much larger flow of information involving countless other individuals. It is openly known that several officers who collaborated with him are still working for the RAW. American reports state that the CIA officials involved were punished for exposing their role. But perhaps again, and more likely, the CIA is not so foolish in exposing themselves after all. It was merely sending a message to other RAW agents : "Betray India and work for us — and if there is any trouble – well absolutely don't worry, both we as well as your own Indian Government will help you"!

Indeed, only just a few months ago, more defectors have followed his path. Not only defectors, but countless other RAW and IB agents have settled down in the US "post-retirement". Is it not true that both Prime Ministers Vajpayee and Manmohan Singh had gone out of their way to protect him? Have not several Prime Ministers in the past exposed critical deep agents of the RAW? Was not our defense minister, Mr. Parikkar, himself forced to admit this?

Does not the example of this cover-up of the Raw defectors by all parties in our government, and that of the Hemant Karkare assassination, and several others post-Karkare (citing ridiculous causes for their deaths), at the highest levels of our country and several other cases besides, show the extent of the infiltration of a Fethullah Gulen-like hydra into India? What are we going to do about it?

Made in the USA
Coppell, TX
26 December 2020